RECIPES FROM

MANY KITCHENS

By VALENTINA RICE

Celebrated Local Food Artisans Share
Their Signature Dishes

PAGE STREET
PUBLISHING CO.

PAGE STREET
PUBLISHING CO.

First published in 2016 by
Page Street Publishing Co.
27 Congress Street, Suite 103
Salem, MA 01970
www.pagestreetpublishing.com

Distributed by Macmillan, sales in Canada by The Canadian Manda Group.

19 18 17 16   1 2 3 4 5

ISBN-13: 9781624142024
ISBN-10: 1624142028

Library of Congress Control Number: 2015948086

Cover and book design by Connie Dickson
Photography by Valentina Rice, styling by Aurora Satler (see page 187 for photography credits)

Printed and bound in the U.S.A.

Page Street is proud to be a member of 1% for the Planet. Members donate one percent of their sales to one or more of the over 1,500 environmental and sustainability charities across the globe who participate in this program.

FOR MY NIGHTINGALES

CONTENTS

INTRODUCTION

"If you can read, you can cook," my mother regularly said in her thick Italian accent. I always thought that was true until I had an epic fail following a celebrity chef's recipe for lamb chops marinated in yogurt. The source, I learned, has a lot to do with the success. Good recipes that never fail you should be collected over time, passed from parent to child, from friend to friend, and treasured as a most prized possession. I learnt this the hard way. A few years back, on a rainy day in November (a Friday, the 13th, no less), I watched the taillights of a cab that contained my suitcase fade away. A pathetic attempt to run after it, a month of trying to locate the driver through the taxi commission and a rather generous reward were all to no avail. Forget the favorite cashmere sweater and the perfectly worn-in pair of jeans; of all the cherished items in my suitcase, it was my recipe book that I longed for the most. Fifteen years of writing and annotating. I felt something akin to a writer losing the only draft of her first novel. The best recipes are worth so much more than any pair of jeans, no matter how good they made my bum look!

My much loved and tattered recipe book contained an approximation of a cherished recipe that my otherwise overly generous grandmother Helen, took to her grave. My paternal grandmother came from what is now Slovakia but then was part of the Austro-Hungarian Empire, and her cooking was influenced by the entire region. Every weekend we visited, she would make the exact same meal of Wiener Schnitzel, mushrooms fried in bread crumbs and the dish in question: marrow (a zucchini-like vegetable) cooked in sour cream and dill. She gave the wrong recipe to my mother time and time again. When my mother finally asked her for the real recipe, she sweetly told her that it was the one dish her grandchildren couldn't get anywhere else and she wanted to keep it that way. She continued to make it for us well into her 90s, and I never smell sour cream and dill without thinking of her and remembering her Sunday lunches.

When the time came to approach my producers to contribute recipes for this book, I did so with trepidation. If my grandmother, a woman so kind that she actually forced money on me to buy my friends new jeans (she was unable to grasp the concept of ripped jeans being a fashion choice), wouldn't share her recipe, what hope did I have of convincing producers to offer theirs?

I had recently given a TEDx talk on the subject of building a community of artisans based on generosity, on sharing resources and on how "competition was so last century," as coined by Claire Marin of Catskill Provisions. The theory proved to be true. My grandmother was born in 1902 and, luckily for me in 2015, the reaction I got from my first hesitant emails asking dozens of artisans for their cherished recipes was unanimously positive! My long-held dream of curating a book of recipes that were as distinctive and reliable as the ones I lost in the cab all those years ago was coming true.

Leaving my job in publishing to create Many Kitchens was the hardest decision I've ever made. Leaving my family and friends to move across the Atlantic to New York seemed like a walk in the park by comparison. Fifteen years of traveling the world and selling books for Penguin had me spending any spare minute I had hunting down the best local specialties and made me near obsessive about doing the same in America. Maybe the impetus behind Many Kitchens began with a jam made from beach plums in Cape Cod that I have never seen anywhere else? What other culinary treasures were hiding across America that deserved a national audience? A casual dinner at a friend's house where ice cream was served that had been shipped from Ohio confirmed that anything can be shipped these days, even ice cream in the middle of summer! From that moment, I couldn't shake the idea of finding the best of the best and creating a virtual community of artisans from across the country that was so much more than the sum of its parts. So, I took a leap off the proverbial cliff and never regretted it for a moment. To then be asked to publish a collection of recipes from these experts in their field was . . . well, I actually have no words to describe how amazing it felt.

As the table of contents began to form into diverse international menus, I felt as if I was holding the keys to the kingdom of magical recipes. The tips that I've learned (and shared) along the way from these incredible artisans—be it the perfect mayonnaise or a rich, smoky mole so versatile it works with almost anything—have made me a better cook and inspired me to try recipes I thought far beyond my abilities. I never believed it possible that I could whip up a batch of perfectly moist madeleines in 20 minutes or roast a pork belly to perfection. So much of cooking is about confidence and breaking down the myth that you have to be trained at a great culinary school to make memorable food. In fact, only a tiny fraction of the artisans we work with at Many Kitchens are professionally trained. Many of them had, like me, left jobs in large companies to follow an unlikely vision of doing what they loved. We work with a banker who now pops corn with his sister, a publisher now making honey and a graphic designer making salsas.

Before launching Many Kitchens, I lacked that confidence, and as a result, stuck to cooking what I knew—which, since my mother is Italian, was pasta and some more pasta. I live in Manhattan, so if I yearned for dumplings or tacos, I simply had to walk a few blocks or pick up the phone to fulfill the craving. After three years of hunting for the best food producers in America and having many of them share their recipes, eating out has lost some of its appeal. Every recipe in this book has been tested in my one-bedroom apartment's tiny galley kitchen on Greenwich Street. Having cooked, recooked and edited every recipe, I can unequivocally say that they are all delicious, reliable and fool-proof. I couldn't be happier to share them with you. I hope this book inspires you to create your own sacred book of favorites much like the one that disappeared up West End Avenue in that yellow cab all those years ago.

A FRENCH BREAKFAST

I was 12 when my father took me on my first trip to Paris. I remember the excitement of visiting a city that seemed impossibly glamorous to my totally unsophisticated self, tasting caviar for the first time and convincing myself I loved it, even if I'm not really sure I did. I was enchanted by our hotel in Saint-Germain-des-Prés that used to be the British ambassador's home and had an elevator with a manual accordion-style brass gate and a beautiful courtyard at the back where breakfast was served. Even now I can vividly picture my father sipping his coffee and reading the International Herald Tribune while I sampled the pain au chocolat, madeleines and croissants and gulped thick hot chocolate before we headed off on foot to explore the city.

It's because of that wonderfully decadent trip, all those years ago, that I wanted an equally decadent French breakfast in this book. The aromas emanating from my kitchen after testing any one of these recipes was enough to transport me to the Hotel d'Angleterre and daydream about returning to taste the croissants that I've yet to match in all their buttery perfection.

MENU

Lavender Hot Chocolate
by Daily Chocolate

Pain Perdu
by Nashoba Brook Bakery

Fig and Port Compote
by Many Kitchens

Buvette's Famous Eggs
by Jody Williams

Tomates Provençales
by Jacqueline et Jerome

Raspberry Madeleines
by Jacqueline et Jerome

LAVENDER HOT CHOCOLATE
by DAILY CHOCOLATE

Makes enough for about 10 servings

A good hot chocolate can warm the cockles of your heart and shouldn't be enjoyed only by children. Using the best-quality chocolate you can find, as Jen Roberts does for her mouthwatering sweets, is crucial to making this recipe stand out. Jen suggests using Guittard or El Rey.

Put the cocoa powder, sugar, chocolate and vanilla into a food processor with a blade attachment and pulse until fairly smooth.

In a saucepan, warm the milk over medium heat and add the lavender buds. When the milk is just steaming with small bubbles at the edge of the pan but not quite boiling, about 5 minutes, strain and return to the pan. Whisk in 2 to 5 tablespoons (30-75 g) of the chocolate mixture. Add more for a richer, thicker beverage or less if you want more of a milk chocolate.

NOTE: Chocolate with a 72% cacao content is ideal, but you can use a mix or lower percentage for a milder flavor. Use disks or small chunks.

2 oz (57 g) organic, undutched, unsweetened cocoa powder

2 oz (57 g) granulated sugar

4 oz (113 g) dark chocolate (see note)

1 tbsp (15 ml) pure vanilla extract

PER SERVING

1 cup (237 ml) whole milk

1 tbsp (10 g) culinary-grade lavender buds

PAIN PERDU
by NASHOBA BROOK BAKERY

Serves 6

6 large eggs

¾ cup (177 ml) half-and-half

¾ cup (177 ml) whole milk

2 tbsp (30 ml) pure vanilla extract

½ tsp ground cinnamon

Pinch of freshly grated nutmeg

Pinch of salt

12 (1"[2.5-cm]) slices of slow-leavened or sourdough bread

9 tbsp (129 g) unsalted butter

Mascarpone cheese, for serving

Fig and Port Compote (page 18)

Unlike English muffins, which are an American invention, French toast is actually French. Slices of the most satisfying, decadent, eggy bread (as it's also known), fried until golden brown, is one of my favorite ways to start the day. Nashoba Brook Bakery makes it with the bakery's own famous Harvest Bread, which is studded with dried fruits and pecans and gives a special twist to the classic dish.

While John Gates of Nashoba Brook Bakery was more than happy to share the recipe for its Harvest Bread, he explained why it is impossible to re-create in a home kitchen. One insurmountable problem is their French bread oven, which is filled with a steam-injected, "cyclothermic" hearth to give the bread consistent moisture and the high temperature necessary to get that perfect crusty loaf. The wild strains of yeast they captured when the bakery was founded in 1998 can't be duplicated. The yeast, nurtured daily, has fed the bakery's doughs ever since.

John told me that when you are buying good artisan bread at a local bakery, there is no universal test for quality; buy what you think tastes good. Nevertheless, it's worth asking, "Is this sourdough naturally yeasted or is commercial baker's yeast used as the main leavening agent?" Old World bread, like Nashoba's, is worth the hunt. It's delicious, nutritious, easy to digest and will stay fresh for a few days longer than even "good" artisan-quality, commercially yeasted bread.

Preheat the oven to 200°F (93°C). Place a baking sheet topped with a wire rack in the middle of the oven.

Whisk together the eggs, half-and-half, milk, vanilla, cinnamon, nutmeg and salt in a large bowl. Whip until the mixture is frothy.

Place the bread in a single layer on a baking sheet with enough of a lip to contain the egg mixture. Pour the egg mixture over the bread and soak for at least 10 minutes. Turn the slices over and leave for at least 10 minutes more, until soggy.

Heat 3 tablespoons (43 g) of the butter in a large skillet over medium-high heat. Add your first four slices of bread. Be sure to wipe any excess egg mixture off the slices before frying; you want them to be nice and soggy but not trailing any of the egg mixture. Fry the bread slices until golden brown, 2 to 3 minutes per side. Transfer to the wire rack.

Wipe the skillet, and repeat with 3 tablespoons (43 g) more of the butter and four more slices of bread. Keep all the cooked bread warm in the oven until ready to serve. Finish the final batch of bread, using the remaining 3 tablespoons (43 g) of butter, and serve warm with mascarpone and the Fig and Port Compote.

FIG AND PORT COMPOTE
by MANY KITCHENS

Makes 1½ cups (225 g) compote

One of the many reasons that August is my favorite time of the year is that the figs become ripe almost overnight. We have a tree at our house in Tuscany that is suddenly so full of sweet, juicy figs that I can pick straight from the low-hanging branches as I pass by. By late August, there are almost too many, and so making a batch of fig compote is the best way to ensure not too many drop to the ground to be eaten by the marauding wild boar. When I first tasted Nashoba Brook's Pain Perdu, I immediately thought how well it would pair with fresh figs or compote. It also goes wonderfully over Greek yogurt and granola for a slightly simpler breakfast.

½ cup (117 ml) port wine

2 tbsp (42 g) honey

1 tbsp (15 ml) freshly squeezed lemon juice

4 oz (113 g) dried figs, stemmed and roughly chopped

½ tsp ground cinnamon

8 oz (230 g) fresh figs, stems removed, quartered

Pinch of sea salt

In a medium-size saucepan over high heat, combine ½ cup (117 ml) of water and the port, honey, lemon juice and dried figs. Bring to a boil, then lower the heat and cook at a low simmer for 10 minutes, allowing the liquid to reduce and the dried figs to begin to soften.

Add the cinnamon, fresh figs and salt. Return to a boil, then lower the heat and simmer for another 5 minutes. The compote is done when the syrup has thickened and the figs are glossy.

Serve at room temperature. The compote will keep, covered and refrigerated, for up to 2 months.

BUVETTE'S FAMOUS EGGS
by JODY WILLIAMS

Serves 1

STEAMED EGGS FOR 1

2 or 3 large eggs

1 tbsp (15 g) unsalted butter

Coarse salt

STOVETOP EGGS FOR 1

2 or 3 large eggs

Coarse salt

2 tbsp (30 g) unsalted butter

2 slices of sourdough bread, toasted

Extra-virgin olive oil, for drizzling

Freshly grated parmesan

Freshly ground black pepper

On a quiet leafy street in the West Village, there is a place that defies categories; it is a restaurant, café and bar all rolled into one. Jody calls it a gastrotèque.

I have followed Buvette's owner, Jody Williams, in near stalkish fashion from my first days in New York when she was the chef at Il Buco in the East Village to her now-growing empire that includes an outpost of Buvette in Paris, as well as a new Italian restaurant, Via Carota, which she opened with her partner, Rita Sodi. Her fava bean and escarole salad is wholly responsible for turning me from a salad avoider to a salad enthusiast. Her steak tartare is the best in the city, as is her croque monsieur. But it is her steamed eggs that secured her status as a true genius in my mind.

The inspiration, she says, came while working for famed chef Thomas Keller at his 1980s New York restaurant, Rakel. One of the signature dishes was mushroom cappuccino, created with steamed milk atop a rich consommé and finished off with grated black truffles. Necessity being the mother of all inventions, Jody began to experiment with the powerful steamer at Gottino on her Faema espresso machine. The result is a plate of the fluffiest eggs imaginable, and I couldn't be more grateful that she has agreed to share them with us.

STEAMED EGGS

Beat all the ingredients together in a tall porcelain jug. Turn the steamer of your espresso machine to full power and release any water into a cup, then discard. Insert the wand into the egg mixture and slowly mix with a fork until the eggs are creamy and soft. Remove just before they're done (after about 30 seconds), as they will keep cooking a bit from the residual heat.

STOVETOP EGGS

Granted, not everyone has a commercial espresso machine at home, so here's how to achieve a similar creamy result on the stove.

Whisk the eggs and salt in a bowl. Set a heavy saucepan over low heat and add half of the butter. Once the butter is melted, add the egg mixture. Using a wooden spoon, continuously scrape the bottom of the pan so that, as the eggs begin to cook, you create a new layer of uncooked egg.

Remove the pan from the heat just before the eggs are ready, between 5 and 10 minutes, as they will continue to cook a little. They should be incredibly creamy and just beginning to set. Add the remaining butter and combine well. Serve immediately on sourdough toast drizzled with olive oil. Sprinkle on some freshly grated Parmesan, a little salt and a few grinds of pepper to finish your eggs.

TOMATES PROVENÇALES
by JACQUELINE ET JEROME

Serves 6

The relatively long cooking time for these tomatoes caramelizes the sugars and gives them an unimaginable tenderness. Make sure to use a baking sheet with a low rim so they don't steam in the pan—you want to get that yummy browning around the edges. I used the leftovers over a bowl of spaghetti with a little extra olive oil and Parmesan—perfect!

This recipe embodies Jerome Bensimon's philosophy of using simple ingredients to create sophisticated, delicious food. When Jerome first sent me a selection of his salad dressings inspired by the ones his grandmother, Jacqueline, made in their native France, I couldn't believe how fresh they tasted. The same is absolutely true for his other family recipes, not least this ideal summer rendering of tomatoes, herbs and garlic.

4 tbsp (60 ml) extra-virgin olive oil

2 lb (907 g) cluster tomatoes (see note)

2 tsp (1 g) herbes de Provence

3 garlic cloves, minced

Sea salt

Preheat the oven to 425°F (218°C). Line a baking sheet with parchment paper and drizzle 1 tablespoon (15 ml) of the oil on it and rub around. Cut the tomatoes in half, making sure to remove any core or tough bits and place on the baking sheet, cut side up. You can also roast still-on-the-vine, for presentation, but the herbs stick better when you cut the tomatoes in half.

Spread the herbs and garlic on the tomatoes, covering them completely. Season with salt and top with the remaining 3 tablespoons (45 ml) of olive oil. Bake the tomatoes for 45 minutes to an hour, until nicely browned and caramelized. Allow to cool for several minutes, then serve warm.

NOTE: Tomatoes on the vine work great; if you want to roast smaller tomatoes, such as cherry tomatoes, just shorten your cooking time by about 15 minutes.

RASPBERRY MADELEINES
by JACQUELINE ET JEROME

Makes about 20 madeleines

4½ oz (127 g) unsalted
butter, plus more for pan

3 large eggs

4½ oz (130 g) granulated sugar

6 oz (170 g) all-purpose flour

¼ tsp baking powder

10-15 raspberries, cut in half

There's no two ways about it: for this recipe you need a madeleine pan, but the fact that, within 20 minutes, you can easily whip up a batch of these soft, buttery French classics should be enough to convince you to get one. You can make them without raspberries if you prefer, but I love the touch of tartness and juiciness that they add.

Preheat the oven to 375°F (190°C).

In a small saucepan, melt the butter and set aside. In a large bowl, beat the eggs and sugar until the mixture becomes pale.

Sift the flour into the bowl, then add the baking powder and melted butter to the mixture. Stir well until smooth.

Butter the madeleine molds well and fill each mold with batter until it is three-quarters full. Nestle a raspberry half in the middle of each one cut side down. Bake for 10 to 15 minutes, until the color is just beginning to turn.

The madeleines will pop right out of their molds and can be served immediately.

A TEX-MEX BRUNCH

Gone are the days of "Tex-Mex" meaning fajitas loaded with sour cream or nachos buried under a mountain of American cheese. The lines between traditional Mexican cuisine and Tex-Mex have blurred so much that the following menu could easily be renamed "Mexican with a modern twist." As with so many cuisines, it has evolved, borrowing from the heritage of regional Mexican cuisine, the bordering regions of Texas and Southern California. Like all great fusion foods, these recipes call for the very best of ingredients. Found anywhere from hipster food trucks to fine-dining restaurants, Tex-Mex should no longer be underestimated.

A few years ago, I visited Austin, Texas, to support friends Camille and Josh who were giving a talk at South by Southwest. My traveling companion was their daughter (and my good friend) Roxie, who good-naturedly cartwheeled her way up and down JFK as we missed all our connections due to snowstorms. When Roxie and I finally arrived, we were picked up by her parents and whisked off to Cheer Up Charlies, a magical bar with fairy lights and food trucks galore. My first experience of Austin, it made me fall in love with the city immediately. Camille and Josh led us through the dancing crowd to sample their discovery of "the most incredible chicken tacos." They were a perfect example of how far Tex-Mex has come—the tacos were as delicious as we'd been led to expect, but shockingly they were not made of actual chicken. The apostrophe in *chick'n* was the red flag for me and it was definitely the only time I'd come that close to being fooled by a vegan substitute!

MENU

Bloody Maria Granita
by Many Kitchens

Fire-Roasted Poblano
Guacamole
by Zukali Mexican Gourmet

Chilaquiles Rojos
by Zukali Mexican Gourmet

Tomatillo Pineapple
Salsa Fresca
by Zukali Mexican Gourmet

Grilled Street Corn
with Chile Salt and Manchego
by the Chili Lab

Tres Leches Cupcakes
by Many Kitchens

BLOODY MARIA GRANITA
by MANY KITCHENS

Makes 4 servings

This is Tex-Mex Italian style! It's a sophisticated slurpy with much more flavor than your average Bloody Mary, thanks to the roasted tomatoes and chipotle peppers in adobo sauce. The tequila replaces vodka in this playful twist on the brunch classic that is part appetizer, part cocktail, part dessert.

Reserving two whole tomatoes, stem, core and slice in half all the other tomatoes.

Preheat the oven to 425°F (218°C). Line a baking sheet with parchment paper and place the sliced tomatoes, cut side up, on the prepared pan. Drizzle with the olive oil, top with the minced garlic and season with celery salt. Bake for 45 minutes to an hour, until nicely browned and caramelized. Meanwhile, blanch the reserved two whole tomatoes in boiling water for 1 to 2 minutes, then peel, core and quarter.

Once the sliced tomatoes have finished roasting, purée both the blanched and roasted tomatoes in a food processor along with the chipotle pepper, adobo sauce, lime juice and black pepper. The blanched tomatoes are a nice addition because they have more juice than the roasted ones, so the combination adds the sweetness of the roasted tomatoes with the fresh, juicier blanched ones. Strain the purée through a sieve and discard any seeds or skins. Then add the basil leaves to the strained mixture and stir well.

Pour the tomato mixture into a wide, shallow container, such as a stainless-steel baking dish (the shallower the container, the quicker the granita will freeze).

Cover with foil or plastic wrap. Freeze the mixture for 1 to 2 hours, until it is solid around the edges. Take the container out of the freezer and scrape the ice with a fork, mixing it from edges into the center and then return the container to the freezer. Repeat the scraping and mixing process at least three times, every 30 minutes or so, until the entire mixture has turned into small, sequined ice flakes. When ready to serve, "rake" with a fork to loosen the granita.

Rim your chosen glass with kosher salt by rubbing the rim with a lime wedge, and once it is wet, dipping the rim into a saucer of kosher salt until coated. If you go for a classic highball, make sure you have tall enough spoons to reach the bottom! Spoon ⅓ cup (80 g) of granita into each rimmed glass. Pour 2 ounces (30 ml) of tequila on top of each granita and serve immediately, garnished with a celery stalk.

NOTE: Season with celery salt as you would with sea salt—the celery salt imparts a slight flavor that is a nice touch for the cocktail later; you can also substitute sea salt if you can't find celery salt.

2 lb (907 g) heirloom tomatoes

3 tbsp (45 ml) extra-virgin olive oil

1 tbsp (10 g) minced garlic

Celery salt (see note)

1 chipotle pepper plus 1 tbsp (14 g) adobo sauce

3 tbsp (45 ml) freshly squeezed lime juice

Freshly ground black pepper

½ cup (20 g) fresh basil leaves

Lime wedge

Kosher salt, for rimming

8 oz (237 ml) tequila

4 celery stalks, for garnish

FIRE-ROASTED POBLANO GUACAMOLE
by ZUKALI MEXICAN GOURMET

Serves 6

2 poblano peppers

3 ripe avocados

½ onion, finely chopped
(about ½ cup [75 g])

3 tbsp (8 g) cilantro leaves,
finely chopped

1 tbsp (15 ml) freshly squeezed
lime juice

1 tsp kosher salt

½ tsp freshly ground black pepper

1 ripe tomato, diced

The roasted poblanos give this guacamole a wonderful smoky flavor. Cesar Sanchez is a master of fire-roasted peppers and salsas that he started making for friends at cookouts in his hometown of McKinney, Texas. They became so popular that he turned them into a successful business, supplying gourmet stores across the country.

Place the poblano peppers directly onto the open flame of your stove. Alternatively, if you do not have a gas stove, you can place them on a baking sheet under the broiler. Using tongs, turn them every 2 to 3 minutes until they are fully charred and blistered all over, about 10 minutes total.

Once charred, place the peppers in a paper or plastic bag, close tightly and let them sweat and cool for about 20 minutes. You should then be able to peel them very easily by using paper towels. Once they are peeled, make a slit down the side of each pepper and remove and discard the cluster of seeds and veins. Finely chop the poblanos.

To make the guacamole, cut the avocados in half, set the pits aside and scoop the avocado flesh into a mixing bowl.

Using a fork or potato masher, mash the avocado. Add the chopped poblanos, onion, cilantro, lime, salt and pepper and mix well. Remember that much of this is done to taste because of the variability in the fresh ingredients. Start with this recipe and adjust the flavorings to your taste.

At this stage you can place the avocado pits on top of the guacamole and cover with plastic wrap, pressed down on the surface to prevent oxidation, and refrigerate. Add the diced tomato just before serving.

CHILAQUILES ROJOS
by ZUKALI MEXICAN GOURMET

Serves 4

When talking over potential recipes for this menu with Cesar Sanchez of Zukali, we discussed various options. My ears pricked up the minute he mentioned chilaquiles, as I'm always excited to learn about dishes that are new to me. It's always nice to be reminded how many regional specialties are still to be discovered and enjoyed. This was no exception; Cesar's smoky salsa, mixed with fried tortilla strips which I like to top with fried eggs, makes the heartiest of brunch dishes and a new favorite for me.

Cut each tortilla in ½-inch (1.3-cm) strips. In a large skillet, heat the vegetable oil over medium-high heat. Add the tortilla strips and fry them for about 2 minutes, moving and turning them frequently until they are golden brown; do not burn. Transfer them to plate lined with paper towels to absorb some of the oil, and set aside.

Remove and discard the seeds and veins from the guajillos. Put the guajillos and tomatoes into a small pot and add enough water to cover. Bring to a boil and let cook for about 5 minutes, until the chiles begin to soften.

Transfer the chiles and tomatoes, plus ¼ cup (60 ml) of the water they cooked in, to a blender. Add half of the chopped onion plus the chipotle pepper, garlic, chicken bouillon powder and pepper to taste. Blend well and set aside.

Heat the olive oil in a saucepan over high heat. Add the salsa you just prepared, and the salt. Wait until the salsa reaches a boil, then lower the heat to medium and simmer for about 15 minutes, until the salsa gets thicker. Lower the heat to low and add the tortilla strips, mixing them slowly in the salsa so not to break them too much. Cook for about 3 minutes, stirring occasionally, until the mixture reaches a thicker consistency; remove from the heat and set aside.

Divide the red chilaquiles among four plates and drizzle with some of the Mexican crema. Add the reserved chopped onion and sprinkle with the queso fresco and cilantro.

Top off each serving with a fried egg and enjoy!

16 corn tortillas (if you have old ones, use those, as they get crunchier when fried)

¾ cup (177 ml) vegetable oil

3 to 4 guajillo chiles

14 oz (400 g) fresh tomatoes, quartered

½ onion, finely chopped

½ chipotle pepper in adobo sauce

1 garlic clove

1 tbsp (6 g) chicken bouillon powder

Freshly ground black pepper

1 tbsp (15 ml) extra-virgin olive oil

1 tsp salt

4 tbsp (30 g) Mexican crema (sour cream)

½ cup (60 g) queso fresco, crumbled

3 oz (85 g) fresh cilantro, finely chopped

4 eggs (fried)

TOMATILLO PINEAPPLE SALSA FRESCA
by ZUKALI MEXICAN GOURMET

Serves 4 to 6

4 fresh pineapple slices

1 lb (483 g) fresh tomatillos, finely diced

1 tbsp (15 ml) pineapple juice

1 tbsp (15 ml) freshly squeezed lime juice

1 tsp sea salt

½ cup (100 g) red onion, finely diced

1 jalapeño pepper, stemmed, deveined, seeded and finely diced (if you want your salsa hotter, include the seeds)

2 tbsp (5 g) finely chopped fresh cilantro

Tortilla chips, for serving

This is a super fresh version of Cesar's delectable jarred Cilantro Pineapple Salsa. You can, of course, blend all the ingredients in a food processor if you prefer a smoother consistency, but I loved how this chunkier version keeps the distinct flavors of the tomatillo and pineapple separate.

Heat a griddle pan over medium-high heat and sear the pineapple slices, 3 to 4 minutes per side. Allow to cool and chop into small cubes.

In a blender, combine half of the tomatillos and the pineapple juice, lime juice and salt. Blend until smooth.

In a medium-size bowl, combine the chopped pineapple, remaining tomatillos, red onion, jalapeño and cilantro along with the puréed tomatillo mixture. Serve with tortilla chips.

GRILLED STREET CORN
WITH CHILE SALT AND MANCHEGO
by THE CHILI LAB

Serves 4

A staple of New York City street fairs and one of my favorite streetside treats, elote is now thankfully as common in America as it is in Mexico. The smell of buttery grilled corn with lime, chile and cheese never fails to lure me to its source. The Chili Lab's addition of Manchego cheese elevates the time-honored recipe to new heights.

In a small bowl, combine the chile powder and sea salt.

Soak the corn ears in their husks for about 20 minutes. Pull back the husks and remove any silks.

Grill the corn over high heat for about 20 minutes, turning regularly to ensure even cooking. (Alternatively, you can also cook these in a preheated oven at 350°F [180°C] for 30 to 35 minutes, turning every 5 minutes.)

Top each of the corn ears with mayonnaise, Manchego, cilantro, lime juice and the chile salt. Serve with lime wedges.

1 tsp chipotle chile powder

1 tsp fine sea salt

4 ears of corn

¼ cup (57 g) mayonnaise

⅓ cup (60 g) finely grated Manchego cheese

2 tbsp (5 g) chopped fresh cilantro

1 tbsp (15 ml) freshly squeezed lime juice

1 lime, cut into 4 wedges

TRES LECHES CUPCAKES
by MANY KITCHENS

Makes 6 cupcakes

CUPCAKES

Nonstick baking spray

1 cup (90 g) unbleached all-purpose flour

1 tsp baking powder

½ tsp salt

5 tbsp (72 g) unsalted butter, at room temperature

¾ cup (144 g) granulated sugar

2 eggs

1 tsp pure vanilla extract

1 cup (237 ml) milk

TRES LECHES

⅔ cup (158 ml) sweetened condensed milk (freeze whatever is left over)

⅓ cup (79 ml) heavy cream

½ cup (118 ml) milk

1 tsp orange liqueur

Zest of 1 lemon

TOPPING

1 cup (237 ml) heavy cream

2 tbsp (30 g) confectioners' sugar

Strips of orange zest

These cupcakes have all the flavor of a classic tres leches cake without the delicious but gooey, milky mess. That means they're great for a party, as you can pick them up without risking a liquid disaster. The orange zest is a crucial touch as it cuts the sweetness of this classic.

MAKE THE CUPCAKES: Preheat the oven to 350°F (180°C). Spray six wells of a nonstick muffin tin with nonstick baking spray.

In a small bowl, whisk together the flour, baking powder and salt.

In a medium-size bowl, cream the butter and sugar until light and fluffy. Add the eggs, one at a time, beating well after each addition. Beat in the vanilla. Mix in one-third of the flour mixture until just incorporated. Follow with half of the milk. Mix in the next third of the flour mixture, then the rest of the milk, and finally beat in the rest of the flour until just incorporated.

Divide the batter evenly among the prepared muffin wells. Bake for 15 to 20 minutes, or until the middle cake bounces back when touched and some of the edges just barely start to turn brown. Allow the cakes to cool slightly in the pan on a wire rack.

MAKE THE TRES LECHES: Mix together all the ingredients in a medium-size bowl and set aside.

Once the cakes have cooled but are still warm, pierce the top of the cupcakes all over with a skewer or toothpick. Pour the tres leches mixture over the warm cakes. Cover and refrigerate until cold, at least 3 hours or overnight.

Use a plastic knife to gently run around the edges of all the cakes to loosen them. Place a large piece of parchment paper over the muffin tin, then top with a large baking sheet. Carefully invert the cakes onto the parchment paper and baking sheet, discarding any extra liquid. Transfer the cupcakes to individual wrappers.

MAKE THE TOPPING: In a small bowl, whip the cream with the confectioners' sugar. Top each cake with a small dollop of whipped cream and a few strips of orange zest.

AN ALL-AMERICAN BBQ

There are many things that I love about living in America, but summer and by extension, the BBQ, rate high on the list. New York has a way of jumping directly from the bitterest of winters to the steamiest of summers with nary a nod to spring. The whiff of smoky meat starts to permeate the air on those first hot days and I find myself longing for Mrs. Bean's burgers. She ran the beach club in Cape Cod, where I've been lucky enough to go since I was a child, and I'm sure I'll never taste a burger quite as juicy as hers. I've been told her secret was an unhealthy amount of butter on the buns, but I think the memory of them has been infused with the carefree happiness of those summers and that is really what makes them unrivaled.

Like many city dwellers, I have no outside space. I have to create menus that can be made and eaten indoors, with only the flavors as a means to transport me to a big summer cookout. All these recipes scream "America" to me and perhaps that's because so many of them were prepared for me the day I was sworn in as an American citizen. To natives they may seem familiar, but each has been worked on and improved by these talented producers to make them better than simply duplicates of classics.

MENU

Peach Rooibos Fizz
by Tay Tea

Short-Rib Sliders
with Bulletproof BBQ Sauce
by Stuart & Co.

Purple Slaw with Lemon
Mayonnaise
by Victoria Amory

Heirloom Beans, Cowboy Style
by Rancho Gordo

Honey Jalapeño Cheddar
Cornbread
by Catskill Provisions

Salted Chocolate
Chip Cookie Sandwich
by Ashley Rodriguez

PEACH ROOIBOS FIZZ
by TAY TEA

Makes 1 drink

Nini makes this thirst-quenching "mocktail" with one of my favorites of her many exquisite blended teas, Kaapstad. Named after the Africaans term for Capetown, it is made with vanilla rooibos, ginger, almond and marigold petals.

Perfect BBQ fare, the peach and mint make this an extra-refreshing nonalcoholic drink. No one's stopping you from adding a splash of gin, to give it an extra kick.

FOR THE SIMPLE SYRUP: In a small saucepan, bring 1 cup (237 ml) of water and the sugar to a boil and let simmer until the sugar is dissolved, about 3 minutes. Remove from the heat and let cool completely.

FOR THE MOCKTAIL: Muddle all the ingredients, except the garnishes, in a cocktail shaker. Shake and strain into an ice-filled glass. Garnish with a peach slice and a sprig of mint.

NOTE: For a ginger flavor, add fresh ginger while making the simple syrup.

SIMPLE SYRUP

1 cup (237 ml) water

1 cup (190 g) granulated sugar

MOCKTAIL

½ peach, cut into thick slices

4 fresh spearmint leaves

1 lemon wedge

2 oz (60 ml) chilled rooibos tea

½ oz (15 ml) simple syrup (see note)

1 oz (30 ml) seltzer

1 spearmint sprig, for garnish

1 thin peach slice, for garnish

SHORT-RIB SLIDERS WITH BULLETPROOF BBQ SAUCE
by STUART & CO.

Makes about 24 sliders

BEEF RUB

¼ cup (60 g) kosher or fine sea salt

3 tbsp (45 g) garlic powder

1 tbsp (15 g) turbinado sugar

1 tbsp (15 g) dried thyme

1 tbsp (15 g) ground ginger

1 tbsp (15 g) chili powder

1 tbsp (15 g) smoked paprika

½ tsp ground cumin

BBQ SAUCE

2 cups (470 ml) cider vinegar

2 cups (250 g) dark brown sugar

1 cup (237 ml) prepared black coffee

1 small yellow onion, puréed in a blender

6 garlic cloves, minced

5 cups (1.2 L) ketchup

SHORT RIBS

2 lb (907 g) boneless short ribs (see note)

¼ cup (25 g) beef rub (recipe above)

2 tbsp (30 g) kosher salt

Grapeseed or vegetable oil

2 cups (470 ml) beef or chicken broth

24 two-bite-size potato buns

At the launch party for Many Kitchens, I wanted to offer food from each of our producers. Michael Steifman of Stuart and Co. memorably brought short rib sliders to showcase his incredible barbecue sauce. They flew off the plates in a matter of minutes and I've been begging for the recipe ever since. I'm so excited that he agreed to share it here.

Michael is living proof that barbecuing is no longer exclusive to the South. His expanding selection of rubs and sauces have saved me on multiple occasions when I find myself with some chicken legs and not much inspiration. His obsession with all things barbecue is forever confirmed in his nickname for his daugher, the most recent addition to his family, Smoky!

MAKE THE BEEF RUB: Combine all the rub ingredients. Store in a cool, dry place.

MAKE THE BBQ SAUCE: Combine the vinegar, brown sugar, coffee, onion and garlic in a saucepot. Bring to a boil, then lower the heat to a simmer and reduce by half, 20 to 30 minutes. Once the liquid has reduced, add the ketchup and whisk until all the ingredients are well combined, then simmer for another 30 minutes, or until the flavor and consistency are to your liking.

PREPARE THE SHORT RIBS: Preheat the oven to 350°F (180°C). Season the short ribs with ¼ cup (25 g) of the beef rub and the kosher salt. Heat a pan or grill to medium-high heat. If using a pan to sear the beef, drizzle the oil in the pan. If using the grill, drizzle the oil on the beef and coat it lightly. Sear the beef on all sides in the pan or on the grill, about 1 minute per side.

Place the short ribs in a Dutch oven or roasting pan large enough for all the ribs to be in one layer. Measure out 2 cups (470 ml) of the BBQ sauce and mix with the beef broth. Pour the mixture over the short ribs until they are just covered. Cover the pot with foil and place in the oven. Braise for 3 hours. Once the ribs are tender and falling apart, remove them from the pan and let them cool. Pour the leftover braising liquid into a saucepot large enough to reheat the shredded beef in. Once the ribs are cool enough to handle, shred them and place them in the sauce. Warm over low heat, then spoon onto the potato buns and serve.

NOTE: You can use bone-in short ribs if that's all you can find; just buy extra to match the bone volume and remove the bones before shredding.

PURPLE SLAW
WITH LEMON MAYONNAISE
by VICTORIA AMORY

Serves 6

It's the bright purple and orange of this super-crunchy coleslaw that makes it my standby. Adding a little vinegar to the shredded vegetables before dressing is a trick my friend Nonie taught me to ensure maximum bite. Using just enough of Victoria Amory's homemade lemony mayonnaise to bind the slaw just before serving keeps it light and fresh.

MAKE THE LEMON MAYONNAISE: In a food processor, purée together the egg, lemon juice and mustard. In a very slow stream, add the olive oil and process until the mayonnaise is thick. Add the salt and taste to adjust the seasonings. Store in an airtight container for no more than a few days.

PREPARE THE SLAW: Remove and discard the hard core of the red cabbage and then slice it lengthwise as thinly as you can (using a mandoline works best). Place in a large bowl. Next, grate the carrots on the largest hole of a box grater or in a food processor with a shredding attachment and add to the bowl. Slice the scallions on the bias and add to the bowl, keeping a third of them aside for garnish. Sprinkle with the vinegar and mix well. Just before serving, add ½ cup (118 g) of the lemon mayonnaise. Mix well, check for seasoning and top with the reserved sliced scallions.

LEMON MAYONNAISE
(MAKES ABOUT 1 CUP [220 G])

1 large egg

2 tbsp (30 ml) lemon juice

¼ tsp Dijon mustard

1 cup (237 ml) olive oil
(not extra-virgin as it has
too strong a flavor)

SLAW

1 medium-size red cabbage

3 carrots

6 scallions

2 tbsp (30 ml) cider vinegar

Salt and freshly ground
black pepper

HEIRLOOM BEANS, COWBOY STYLE
by RANCHO GORDO

Serves 6

8 oz (225 g) dried Rio Zape, Moro, Yellow Indian Woman or cranberry beans

1 bay leaf

2 strips of bacon, chopped into large squares

Extra-virgin olive oil (optional)

½ white onion, peeled and chopped

2 garlic cloves, peeled and smashed

2 red bell peppers, seeded and roughly chopped

1 tsp Indio oregano (Mexican oregano)

1 tsp fresh thyme

Salt

Beer (optional)

This side dish is so flavorful and hearty that you could happily eat it as a thick soup all on its own. It's worth making the effort to find heirloom beans, as not only does it make a world of difference to the taste, but it also dramatically reduces the cooking time.

Like heirloom tomatoes, heirloom beans often have more complex, interesting texture and flavors. You could make a dish like this with chicken stock, but heirlooms don't need much help, and the secret is to stand back and let them take center stage. Beans last for years in a pantry, but they're really best within two years of harvest. Steve Sando of Rancho Gordo has made it his mission to educate the world on heirloom beans by working with farmers in Mexico to make sure that indigenous crops and older varieties of beans survive.

Rinse the beans with lots of cool water and inspect them for pebbles or other organic debris. Place the cleaned beans in a medium-size stockpot and cover by about 2 inches (5 cm) of cold water. Add the bay leaf. Bring to a boil over high heat and allow the beans to boil rapidly for about 15 minutes. Lower the heat to low so the beans can continue cooking at a gentle simmer. The beans should start to soften after an hour.

Meanwhile, cook the bacon in a sauté pan. When the bacon is crispy, about 5 minutes, transfer it to paper towels, reserving all the bacon fat in the pan. Your goal is about 2 tablespoons (30 g) of fat. Discard the excess or add olive oil if needed. Sauté the onion and garlic in the bacon fat until just soft, about 5 minutes. Add the bell peppers, oregano and thyme and cook for another 6 minutes. The vegetables should be thoroughly cooked but not falling apart. Remove from the heat and let rest until the beans are cooked.

Once the beans are soft but not quite cooked through, add the salt and stir. Continue to cook until the beans are soft. Add the vegetable mixture and stir gently. The beans should be surrounded by liquid but not too watery or dry. When you take a spoonful, you want nice soft beans and a little bit of liquid that has thickened slightly while cooking to about the consistency of a thin pea soup. Add some beer if you find you need more liquid or want to it add for flavor. Just before serving, stir in the reserved bacon.

(continued)

COOKING BEANS: TO SOAK OR NOT TO SOAK
by STEVE SANDO

Traditionally, chefs who cook beans have been told to soak the raw beans overnight in cold water. When it's time to cook, the advice is to strain the beans and add fresh water and then start cooking. This isn't a bad idea, especially if you don't know where your beans are coming from. Supermarket beans can easily be older than your school-age children! If you are buying from a grower that you know and trust, such as Rancho Gordo, your beans are less than two years old, and more often less than one. This means they cook faster (and most likely taste better) than anything you'd find in your average supermarket. It also means you don't really have to soak them. In India and Mexico, most cooks just throw the beans, water and some aromatics into a pot and start cooking, and it's worked for them for centuries.

Some folks will tell you that soaking and discarding the soaking water will make the beans more digestible (if you know what I mean?). Others say that the effect is minimal and that to make beans more digestible, you need to eat them more often and get your system acclimated to a high-fiber diet. At Rancho Gordo, we say you should do what you like. We've made thousands of pots of beans and 90 percent of the time we don't soak and no one seems to have suffered.

HONEY JALAPEÑO CHEDDAR CORNBREAD
by CATSKILL PROVISIONS

Serves 4-6

Everything a cornbread should be and more. Moist and crumbly with a touch of heat and sweetness. This is perfect to serve with your cowboy beans, to mop up the extra sauce.

Preheat the oven to 375°F (190°C). Mix together the cornmeal, flour, baking powder, paprika and salt. Stir in the cheese. In a smaller bowl, whisk together the buttermilk, vegetable oil, eggs, jalapeños and honey. Slowly add the buttermilk mixture to the cornmeal mixture, stirring just until moistened.

Butter a baking dish—I used a square one, 8 x 8 inches (20 x 20 cm)—and spoon in the batter. Bake for 20 to 25 minutes, or until golden and a toothpick inserted into the center comes out clean. Remove from the pan and let cool on a wire rack. Serve warm with extra honey for drizzling.

1 cup (170 g) yellow cornmeal

1 cup (170 g) all-purpose flour

1 tbsp (11 g) baking powder

½ tsp hot smoked paprika

¾ tsp salt

2 cups (240 g) grated sharp cheddar cheese

1 cup (237 ml) buttermilk

¼ cup (60 ml) vegetable oil

2 large eggs

2 jalapeño peppers, stemmed and seeded, cut into small dice

3 tbsp (64 g) honey, plus more for drizzling

1½ tsp unsalted butter, for pan

SALTED CHOCOLATE CHIP COOKIE SANDWICH
by ASHLEY RODRIGUEZ

Makes 18 to 24 cookies (9 to 12 sandwiches)

½ cup (115 g) unsalted butter, at room temperature

2 tbsp (25 g) granulated sugar

2 tbsp (25 g) turbinado sugar

¾ cup plus 2 tablespoons (175 g) packed dark brown sugar

1 large egg, at room temperature

1 tsp pure vanilla extract

1¾ cups (250 g) all-purpose flour

¾ tsp baking soda

½ tsp kosher salt

6 oz (170 g) bittersweet chocolate, cut into ½" (1.3 cm) chunks with a serrated knife

Flake salt, such as Maldon, for finishing

Vanilla ice cream

To say that Ashley's chocolate chip cookies are the best I've ever made is a terrible understatement. Her cookies have become so famous that she started selling the mix and, before long, it became one of our best sellers at Many Kitchens. All the ingredients are perfectly measured out, including a mini bag of salt crystals that put the finishing touch on these gooey, chewy beauties. I did have some serious explaining to do when a friend found said bag on my coffee table and thought I had become a crystal meth addict! Turning these cookies into an ice-cream sandwich is just an excuse to eat two at a time!

In a medium-size bowl, cream the butter and sugars together with an electric mixer on medium speed until light in color and texture, about 5 minutes. Scrape down the sides of the bowl with a rubber spatula as needed. Add the egg and vanilla and mix well. Again, scrape the sides with a spatula.

In a separate medium-size bowl, whisk together the flour, baking soda and salt. With the mixer on low speed, slowly add the flour mixture to the butter mixture. Then add the chocolate and mix until everything is combined. Finish the dough by hand and make sure everything is evenly distributed.

At this point, you should refrigerate the dough for 24 hours. Resting the dough will intensify the flavors and the texture of the baked cookie will improve.

When ready to bake, preheat the oven to 360°F (182°C). Line two baking sheets with parchment paper and scoop the dough 1 inch (2.5 cm) apart onto the prepared baking sheets. Top the cookies with a pinch of flake salt just before baking. Bake for 10 to 12 minutes, rotating the sheets halfway through if they appear to be baking unevenly. The cookies should be lightly golden brown on the outside but still look gooey on the inside. Let cool on the pans for at least 5 minutes before transferring to a wire rack to finish cooling.

To assemble your sandwiches, take a large scoop of ice cream and gently squish between two cookies. If you're making a platterful, you can freeze them for about 10 minutes before laying out for eager fingers.

AN ENGLISH TEA

Woe betide anyone who tries to get between the English and their cup of tea! I think the most commonly used phrase in the English language might very well be "I'll pop the kettle on." Sadly, though, a full English tea is not as common as it used to be and is something reserved for special occasions.

I remember being taken as a child to Claridge's, a hotel in Mayfair, famous for its afternoon tea. I think the memory is such a vivid one as we were going to meet some friends of my father's who were visiting from Peru, a country I knew nothing about, save knowing it as the home of Paddington Bear. I remember asking whether they knew Paddington Bear and not understanding why that might be funny. It's my first memory of a proper English tea with all the trimmings: Beautiful plates piled high in tiered silver serving racks full of perfect finger sandwiches with the crusts all cut off, just the way I liked them. Scones fresh from the oven with clotted cream as thick as butter. All very formally served by men in tails. The next time I experienced such a lavish tea was over 30 years later in New York City; the occasion was a discussion of this very chapter. The menu pays homage to that tea at Claridge's as well as the more recent one at Lady Mendl's, and I can only hope that afternoon tea makes a comeback so I don't have to wait another 30 years.

MENU

Madeira Cake
by British Baking Company

Currant Scones
by Nashoba Brook Bakery

Afternoon Tea Strawberry Jam
by Hillhome Country Products

Smoked Salmon Mousse and
Quick Pickled-Cucumber
Tea Sandwiches
by Many Kitchens

Coronation Chicken Tea
Sandwiches by Many Kitchens

THE ENGLISH AND THEIR TEA
WITH IN PURSUIT OF TEA

Over the course of the most extravagant tea of my life, I grilled "tea guru" (and founder of In Pursuit of Tea) Sebastian Beckwith about the real story behind the English and their obsession with tea. We met at Lady Mendl's, a tearoom on Irving Place, lovingly and lusciously designed by owner Sarah Blumenthal. Between mouthfuls of buttermilk scones with thick clotted cream and perfect, crustless finger sandwiches, Sebastian, a purist but by no means a militant, generously educated me and kindly refrained from voicing disapproval when I put milk and sugar in my tea.

I learned that tea came from China to England in the 1600s. It was so wildly popular that to import it to England and not drain the royal coffers, the British had to trade in opium to get more silver, which they in turn used to buy more tea. It wasn't until the 1800s that tea was produced in the Indian subcontinent. A Scotsman named Robert Fortune, disguised as a Chinese man, smuggled some twenty thousand Chinese tea plants (and, indeed, Chinese workers) to Darjeeling—a topic controversial in Assam, where locals will tell you that tea plants are indigenous to the region and were around long before the 1800s. The history of tea is endlessly fascinating and forever linked to politics. In fact, it is as a result of the infamous Boston Tea Party that the tea culture in the United States largely perished, as tea became associated with loyalty to England.

History complete, we moved to the beverage itself. "English Breakfast tea," which ironically is globally ubiquitous except in England, turns out to mean nothing more than a blend of any black teas. In answer to the age-old question, milk first or after, Sebastian quoted his good friend the Thane of Cawdor: "Only ever after, as in happily or milkily." I received an equally charming response to the question of how long you should brew your tea: "Until it's the way you like it."

Heating the pot, on the other hand, has a practical rationale of not reducing the temperature of the water as soon as it's added. I was gratified to hear that historically, only the well-to-do could afford sugar, so I now have a response the next time my friends in England mock me for my heaped teaspoon. (Adding sugar is considered "common" in England and tea connoisseurs think it destroys the delicate taste of the tea.)

After two hours, there was still so much more I wanted to learn. But two hours at Lady Mendl's is time well spent. After six courses ending in Lady M's (no relation) famous Mille Crêpe Cake, we couldn't eat another scrumptious bite. I will have to wait until I see Sebastian again to continue my education on this leaf that has affected global politics for over 400 years.

MADEIRA CAKE
by BRITISH BAKING COMPANY

Makes 1 (8 x 4-inch [20 x 10-cm]) loaf

6 oz (170 g) unsalted butter, plus more for pan

6.3 oz (179 g) superfine sugar

Zest of 1 orange

Zest of 1 lemon

4 large eggs

1 tbsp (15 ml) freshly squeezed lemon juice

6 oz (170 g) all-purpose flour, plus more for pan

½ tsp kosher salt

1 tsp baking powder

Apricot jam

1 tsp water

My parents were neither English by birth nor particularly sweet toothed but for some reason, there was always a Madeira cake in the fridge. Its name comes only from the fact that it was eaten alongside Madeira wine. Similar to a classic pound cake, it doesn't look like anything special until you start eating and just can't stop. I feel the same way about Madeira cake as John D. Rockefeller did about money. "How much money is enough?" someone famously asked him. "Just a little bit more," he replied.

This Madeira cake is even better than the one I remember loving so much as a child and it is a real treat to have the recipe. I first met British Baking Company's Wendy Taylor, in true New York style, through my yoga teacher. We were both just starting out building our businesses and our first meeting consisted of a trip down memory lane for both of us as we listed our favorite English sweets. Each was followed by a mutual sigh and a rumbling of the stomach. "Sticky toffee pudding," "treacle tart," "flapjacks," "Madeira cake," and on and on we went. The following week, Wendy arrived at my house with samples galore and I was instantly transported back to England and all the foods I hadn't realized I was missing.

Preheat the oven to 325°F (163°C). Have all the ingredients at room temperature.

Using an electric mixer on medium speed, beat the butter, sugar and zests until fluffy. Add the eggs one at a time. Then add the lemon juice. In a medium-size bowl, sift the dry ingredients together and then fold into the butter mixture. Don't overmix.

Butter and flour a standard 8 x 4-inch (20 x 10-cm) loaf pan. Spoon the batter into the pan. Level the top with a spatula or spoon. Bake for about an hour, until a tester comes out clean and free of crumbs. I use a wooden skewer to test. If the cake seems to be browning too quickly, loosely cover the top with foil. Once baked, without removing it from its pan, place the cake on a wire rack to cool. Allow it to rest for about 10 minutes.

Make a glaze by heating the apricot jam and 1 teaspoon of water in a small saucepan over medium heat until the consistency is just liquid enough to brush on the cake, about 5 minutes.

As the cake is resting, carefully brush with the apricot glaze. Once the cake has cooled, gently run a spatula along the cake pan sides and invert the cake to remove it from the pan.

NOTE: The cake tastes better the next day. Wrap, and it will keep for about 4 days at room temperature or for about a week refrigerated. Bring to room temperature before serving.

CURRANT SCONES
by NASHOBA BROOK BAKERY

Makes 8 scones

I still can't get over how moist and flaky these scones are. Topped with clotted cream and strawberry jam, they are decadent and gratifying. The most important lesson I learned while testing this recipe was to check the expiration date of your baking powder—it really does stop working! If in doubt, put a teaspoon into hot water and, if it fizzes, you're good to go.

Combine the bread flour, cake flour, sugar, salt and baking powder in a stand mixer or use a handheld mixer in a large bowl. Add the butter and mix on low speed until the texture is like sand; do not overmix.

Add the cream and mix at slow speed until the ingredients come together; again, do not overmix. Add the currants and mix until the fruit is evenly distributed. Lay out a sheet of plastic wrap and scrape the contents of the bowl onto it. Wrap the dough in the plastic and refrigerate for at least 2 hours.

Preheat the oven to 320°F (160°C).

While the dough is chilling, lightly grease a sheet pan or cookie sheet. The butter wrapper works really well for this. Place the dough on a floured surface and roll out until it is 1 inch (2.5 cm) thick. If the dough starts to stick, dust the rolling pin and surface of the mixture with flour.

Using a 3-inch (7.5-cm) circular cutter (a cookie cutter or a small glass can work well), cut out the scones and place on the prepared pan. Brush with the beaten egg and bake for about 45 minutes, or until golden brown on top. Transfer to a wire rack to cool.

8½ oz (240 g) unbleached bread flour

3 oz (85 g) cake flour

3 oz (85 g) granulated sugar

½ tsp salt

1 tbsp (6 g) baking powder

8 oz (227 g) unsalted butter, chilled and cubed (reserve wrapper for greasing pan)

7 oz (220 ml) heavy cream

4 oz (113 g) currants or raisins

1 large egg, whisked

AFTERNOON TEA
STRAWBERRY JAM
by HILLHOME COUNTRY PRODUCTS

Makes 1 pint (475 g) jam

I came across David Davis at a farmers' market in Connecticut. A distinguished Englishman in a bow tie, selling jars of both classic preserves as well as innovative new ones, he had me hooked from the first taste of his Vidalia Onion Jam that I'm now addicted to. In fact, I have a fridge filled with his jams, including this absolute classic.

David uses only the freshest of strawberries for his jam. Run out and get them the minute you first see them at the farmers' market. Once you've made this recipe, you can enjoy that fresh taste all year round.

Wash two half-pint (237 ml) jars thoroughly in soapy water. Rinse, drain and place, open end up, on a sheet pan. Dry in a 225°F (107°C) oven for at least 10 minutes. This will sterilize the jars. The caps and rings should be immersed in water in a saucepan and brought just to a boil. Do not prolong the boiling. You will damage the plastisol coating and risk not creating a good seal at bottling time.

Lower the oven temperature to 150°F (67°C) or as low as it will go.

Rinse and hull the strawberries. If the strawberries are larger than a thumbnail, cut them into quarters. Place the strawberries in a large, heavy-bottomed pot.

Add the lemon juice and pectin. Over medium to high heat, bring to a rolling boil, stirring frequently. While the pectin mixture is coming to a boil, warm the sugar in the 150°F (67°C) oven. Add half of the sugar to the pectin mixture. Bring back to a boil. Add the rest of the sugar.

Bring back to a rolling boil. Set a timer for 3 minutes. Check for setting after 2 minutes. Allow to sit for 10 minutes before bottling. Skim off all foam during this time.

Remove the jars from the oven and allow them to sit on the sheet pan. This will allow them to cool slightly so that strawberry jam will not boil when it is ladled into the jars. Ladle carefully into your jars, leaving a ½-inch (1.3-cm) space at the top of each jar. Check to see that the top of each jar is free of any jam. If necessary, wipe the rim with a clean, damp paper towel. With tongs, remove the lids from the water, drain and place on top of the jars. Screw on the rings to create a proper seal.

Invert the filled jars for 10 minutes to allow the fruit to disperse evenly through the jars—but only for 10 minutes, otherwise you may make an improper seal. Return the jars to an upright position and leave them to cool and set overnight.

The next day, the jam may be labeled, dated and stored in a cool place.

1 lb (453 g) strawberries

Juice of 1 lemon

2 oz (55 g) powdered pectin (see note)

3½ level cups (670 g) granulated sugar

NOTE: Powdered pectin is readily available online and at stores where preserving products are sold, but you can also use liquid pectin if that is more accessible—just follow the instructions on the packet.

SMOKED SALMON MOUSSE AND QUICK PICKLED-CUCUMBER TEA SANDWICHES

by MANY KITCHENS

Makes 8 to 10 sandwiches

This is a wonderful mousse to make extra of and serve with crackers, as it lasts for a while in the fridge. The quick pickled cucumber adds just the right amount of acidity and crunch to the sandwich to balance the creaminess of the mousse. Prepare it the night before you plan to serve the sandwiches.

PREPARE THE PICKLED CUCUMBER: Slice the cucumber on a mandoline set to 1/16 inch (1.5 mm). In a small, sealable plastic container, combine remaining ingredients with the cucumber, fasten the lid and give it a good shake. Refrigerate overnight.

PREPARE THE SALMON MOUSSE: In a food processor, mix the cream cheese, horseradish and lemon juice. Once combined, add the chopped salmon and dill and pulse to your liking.

ASSEMBLE THE SANDWICHES: On a slice of pumpernickel bread, spread a generous amount of smoked salmon mousse. Next, add a layer of cucumber slices that overlap where they intersect. Add smoked salmon and top with another slice of pumpernickel. Cut off the crusts and slice your sandwich with a sharp knife into triangles or long rectangles. Serve immediately.

NOTE: If you are laying out sandwiches in advance, top with a slightly damp paper towel until your guests arrive, so the bread does not become stale.

QUICK PICKLED CUCUMBER

1 Persian cucumber

1 tbsp (3 g) chopped fresh dill

¼ tsp coarse kosher salt

¼ cup (60 ml) rice vinegar

SMOKED SALMON MOUSSE

7 oz (200 g) cream cheese, softened

1 tsp prepared horseradish

Juice of 1 lemon

5 oz (142 g) smoked salmon, chopped

1 tbsp (3 g) chopped fresh dill

TO ASSEMBLE

Pumpernickel bread

Smoked salmon

CORONATION CHICKEN TEA SANDWICHES

by MANY KITCHENS

Serves 6

2 chicken breasts

1 tbsp (6 g) curry powder

1 tsp Worcestershire sauce

¼ cup (60 g) Greek yogurt

¼ cup (60 g) mayonnaise

3 tbsp (46 g) good-quality mango chutney

¼ cup (40 g) golden raisins

½ cup (20 g) chopped fresh cilantro

½ cup (85 g) sliced almonds, toasted

12 slices good-quality white bread

Coronation chicken has been a British staple since Queen Elizabeth's coronation in 1953. Curry powder was difficult to come by in postwar Britain, so this dish was considered a decadent luxury. I love the mix of flavors with sweet, savory and a touch of heat from the curry; it's a nod to the waning British colonies.

In a saucepan, bring to a slow boil enough water to cover the chicken by 1 inch (2.5 cm). Season the chicken breasts and add to the water. Keep at a low simmer and poach the chicken until cooked through, about 15 minutes.

Meanwhile, in a bowl, mix together all the other ingredients, except the bread. When the chicken is done, leave it to cool and then shred it with two forks. Once fully cooled, add to the mixture and mix well. You can make this in advance and just spoon onto your choice of good bread. Assemble into sandwiches and cut the crusts cut off.

A SOUTHERN SUMMER PICNIC

Not long after moving to America, I visited friends in Fredericksburg, Virginia. My knowledge of the South until then was based on a mixture of Scarlett O'Hara and John Boy Walton, so I wasn't sure what to expect. What I discovered is that they call it a "Southern welcome" for a reason. I was plied with copious quantities of delicious food and sweet iced tea while being introduced to my friend's large extended family on the obligatory wraparound porch with its swinging bench. Christopher's mother, Linda, grew up in Savannah, Georgia, and was exactly as I had imagined a true southern belle would be: Utterly charming and elegant, she proclaimed everything (including me) to be "just precious." It is her famous peach pie that she generously shared with me which is included in this menu.

The next day, we spent the morning tubing down the Rappahannock River, which ended in a slightly embarrassing rescue by Christopher's brother Schuyler, after I got stuck in what felt like a rapid but was probably more like a gentle ripple. Christopher's honor at stake, he maintains to this day that he was too far downstream to help me. We went on to visit all the local attractions, including the houses of more than a few of George Washington's relatives, and then enjoyed a lot more food before happily driving back to New York. As an introduction to the South, I could not have asked for more.

MENU

Mint Julep
by Catskill Provisions

Kickin' Corn Relish
by Hillhome Country Products

Fried Chicken Sandwich
by Ashley Rodriquez

Vanilla Caramel Popcorn
by the Caramel Jar

Sugar and Spice Pecans
by La Canne Sugar Products

Georgia Peach Pie
by Linda LeHardy Sweet

MINT JULEP
by CATSKILL PROVISIONS

Makes 1 drink

I never doubted the drink that I wanted to go along with this slightly sinful menu. Quite apart from the fact that nothing says "Southern summer" to me like mint juleps, they are delightful and refreshing, and I love that they have their very own, instantly recognizable cup.

The official drink of the Kentucky Derby, some 120,000 juleps are served each year at Churchill Downs. By my estimation, that's over 7,000 liters of bourbon!

MAKE THE MINTED SIMPLE SYRUP: In a saucepan over medium heat, stir together 1 cup (237 ml) of water and the sugar until the sugar dissolves. Simmer for 5 minutes, stirring occasionally. Remove from the heat, add the mint and leave to steep for 15 minutes. Strain, then refrigerate the syrup until cold.

PREPARE THE MINT JULEP: Place 1 ounce (30 ml) of the minted simple syrup, then 1 cup (228 g) of the crushed ice, the bourbon and a splash of water in a silver julep cup or highball glass. Add enough of the remaining ice to almost fill the glass. Stir well and garnish with the mint sprig.

MINTED SIMPLE SYRUP
(MAKES 1½ CUPS [355 ML])

1 cup (190 g) granulated sugar

1 bunch fresh mint

PER JULEP

1 oz (30 ml) minted simple syrup

2 cups (455 g) crushed ice

2 oz (60 ml) bourbon

Fresh mint sprig, for garnish

KICKIN' CORN RELISH
by HILLHOME COUNTRY PRODUCTS

Makes 5 to 6 cups (1,200-1,440 g)

½ cup (118 ml) white wine vinegar

¼ cup (48 g) granulated sugar

¼ tsp ground cumin

½ tsp salt

¼ tsp red pepper flakes

2 poblano peppers

5 ears of corn

½ cup (75 g) red finely diced onion

½ cup (75 g) red bell pepper finely diced

½ jalapeño pepper, finely diced

¾ cup (150 g) black beans, cooked and drained (optional)

The ideal accompaniment to any picnic or cookout, this relish has just the right amount of bite and acidity to cut through the richness of fried chicken. It's also another great use of that perfect, but fleeting, summer corn. Preserving it gives you weeks more of enjoyment.

Combine the vinegar, sugar, cumin, salt and red pepper flakes in a small saucepan.

Bring to a boil, remove from the heat and set aside.

Broil the poblano peppers until well blackened on all sides, turning as needed.

Place the broiled peppers in a bowl and cover with plastic wrap. Sweat the peppers for 10 to 15 minutes. Remove from the bowl, peel off the skins, remove and discard the seeds and chop.

Remove the husks and silk from the corn. Place in boiling water for 5 minutes, then transfer to an ice water bath to stop the cooking. Scrape the corn kernels from the cob into a bowl. Add the poblano peppers, red onion, red bell pepper, jalapeño and beans (if using) to the corn.

If the vinegar mixture has cooled, warm it again. Add the warm liquid to the vegetables in the bowl. Mix all the ingredients well and let stand at room temperature until cool.

When cool, refrigerate for at least 1 day (and up to three) before serving.

FRIED CHICKEN SANDWICH
by ASHLEY RODRIGUEZ

Serves 4

I've been a fan of Ashley's blog Not Without Salt for a long time. Her incredible success couldn't be more well deserved. Not only does she write with great charm and take the most mouthwatering of photos, but she is able to take classic recipes to new heights in the most unexpected ways. This fried chicken is an ideal example of that talent. The secret lies in brining the chicken overnight in a salt and spice rub that makes the chicken extra crispy.

MAKE THE SPICE MIX: The day before you plan on frying the chicken, whisk together all the ingredients for the spice mix. Set 1 tablespoon (6 g) aside and sprinkle the rest all over the chicken thighs. Cover the chicken with plastic wrap and refrigerate overnight.

PREPARE THE CHICKEN: Preheat the oven to 375°F (190°C).

In a shallow dish, mix together the buttermilk and egg. In a separate shallow dish, mix together the flour, cornstarch, baking powder and the reserved spice mix.

Place a wire rack over a sheet pan. Fill a large, heavy skillet, such as a 12-inch (30.5-cm) cast-iron pan, with ¾ inch (2 cm) of canola oil. Over high heat, bring the oil to 360°F (182°C).

Dredge the chicken in the buttermilk mixture, then in the flour mixture, then in the buttermilk mixture again and finally back in the flour mixture. Set each piece on the wire rack once fully dredged.

Fry the chicken for 3 minutes per side, until deep golden brown. Clean the wire rack of the dredging residue, return the chicken to the rack and bake for a further 8 to 10 minutes, or until just cooked inside.

MAKE THE WAFFLES: Beat together the eggs, milk, butter and ½ cup (118 ml) of water in a large bowl. Add the flour, baking powder and salt and blend well until there are no lumps. Heat your waffle maker, spray with cooking spray or brush with oil and pour in some batter when it's ready, spreading out from the center. The amount of batter and time depends on your waffle iron. Once your waffles are nicely browned, pop them out and place a piece of fried chicken between two of them. I like to drizzle honey on the chicken, which I'm assured is the Southern way!

SPICE MIX

1 tsp smoked paprika

1 tsp dried oregano

1 tsp dried thyme

1 tsp dried marjoram

1 tsp garlic powder

½ tsp freshly ground black pepper

2 tsp (10 g) kosher salt

CHICKEN

4 boneless, skinless chicken thighs

1 cup (240 ml) buttermilk

1 large egg

1 cup (140 g) all-purpose flour

1 tbsp (5 g) cornstarch

½ tsp baking powder

4 cups (946 ml) canola, vegetable or peanut oil

WAFFLES

2 large eggs

1½ cups (355 ml) whole milk

2 tbsp (29 g) unsalted butter, melted

10 oz (284 g) stone-ground whole wheat flour

½ tsp baking powder

½ tsp salt

Cooking spray or oil, for waffle iron

Honey (for drizzling)

VANILLA CARAMEL POPCORN
by THE CARAMEL JAR

Makes roughly 8 to 10 cups (719-900 g) popcorn

½ cup (46 g) popcorn kernels

8 tbsp (115 g) unsalted butter

1 tsp fleur de sel

1 cup (200 g) lightly packed brown sugar

¼ cup (60 ml) brown rice syrup or light corn syrup

1½ tsp (7 ml) pure vanilla extract

¼ tsp baking soda

This popcorn is so ridiculously addictive, I've had to give what was left of my stash away. No matter how many times I put it to the back of the cupboard, I find myself rummaging around for just another handful of these enticingly sweet and crunchy treats.

Make the popcorn (if you don't have an air popper, use a large saucepan with a tight-fitting lid). Remove any unpopped kernels and set aside in large, heatproof mixing bowl.

Preheat the oven to 275°F (135°C).

Combine the butter, fleur de sel, brown sugar, brown rice syrup and vanilla in a saucepan over medium-high heat. Stir gently until it comes to a rolling boil and the sugar mixture starts to change color and fluff up, or reaches 230°F (110°C) on a candy thermometer. Remove the sugar mixture from the heat. Add the baking soda and pour the mixture over the popcorn. Mix gently until well coated. Spread on parchment-lined baking sheets and bake for 45 minutes, stirring every 15 minutes. Remove from the oven and give a final mix on the baking sheets to reincorporate the caramel that has melted off. Spread out on the same baking sheets, give it a final stir, and let cool. Once cool, store in an airtight container for 4 to 7 days. If it lasts that long!

SUGAR AND SPICE PECANS
by LA CANNE SUGAR PRODUCTS

Makes about 2 cups (242 g) pecans

I love the combination of the sweet and salty with a touch of heat from this recipe. The roasting and the blend of sugar and spices elevate the already tasty pecan to a sophisticated snack. Fill a mason jar with these pecans and they make a wonderful hostess gift. Tony Bonomolo and Gabriel Senette got the idea to smoke Louisiana cane sugar over pecan shells to get the flavor infused. They started their company with pecan-smoked sugar to such success that they went on to include lavender and then ginger.

Preheat the oven to 350°F (180°C).

In a large bowl, combine the melted butter with the brown sugar, salt and spices. Mix well, then add the pecans and stir until they are fully coated. Bake the pecans on an ungreased cookie sheet for 10 minutes. Remove from the oven and sprinkle with an extra pinch of sea salt.

Allow to cool, then serve.

2 tbsp (30 ml) unsalted butter, melted

2 tbsp (25 g) coarse brown sugar

1 tsp sea salt, plus a pinch for sprinkling

½ tsp sweet smoked paprika

½ tsp cayenne pepper

8 oz (227 g) whole, shelled pecans

GEORGIA PEACH PIE
by LINDA LEHARDY SWEET

Makes 1 (9-inch [23-cm]) pie

PIECRUST

2 cups (180 g) all-purpose flour, plus more for dusting

1 tsp salt

14 tbsp (200 g) unsalted butter, chilled

4 to 6 tbsp (60 to 90 ml) ice water

FILLING

2 lb (907 g) fresh peaches (about 10), pits and skin removed and sliced, or frozen peaches, sliced and well thawed

1 tbsp (15 ml) freshly squeezed lemon juice

½ cup (96 g) granulated sugar

¼ cup (22 g) all-purpose flour

Pinch of sea salt

2 tbsp (30 g) unsalted butter

1 egg for wash

The perfectly flaky, all-butter crust is what really makes this Southern peach pie sing. To find the best Georgia peach pie recipe, I went right to the source. My friend Christopher's mother comes from an old Savannah family and she kindly shared her beloved recipe.

Preheat the oven to 425°F (218°C).

MAKE THE PIECRUST: Combine the flour, salt and butter in a standing mixer. If you only have a handheld mixer, that will work as well. Mix until the consistency is similar to that of grainy sand.

Once you've mixed in the butter, add the cold water, tablespoon by tablespoon. You want a dough that will just stick together once you press it into a ball, without leaving clumps of flour behind. Once the dough is wet enough to form a ball, divide in half. Cover one portion with plastic wrap and refrigerate. For your other half, roll out on a floured surface until the dough is an inch (2.5 cm) larger than the widest part of your pie pan. When rolling out, be sure to flour your rolling pin and also to flip the dough over so that it doesn't start to stick to your surface. Gently fold your rolled dough in half and then fold in half once more. Lay inside a standard 9-inch (23-cm) pie pan and unfurl all the sides, letting any extra crust drape over the sides. Press to the sides of the pan and fold the excess crust back under itself.

Cut a circle of parchment paper that fits over your crust. Fill the lined crust with pie weights (uncooked beans work as well if you don't have weights). Bake the crust until the edges are just slightly brown, 10 to 12 minutes. Remove from the oven and allow to cool completely before filling.

PREPARE THE FILLING: In a large bowl, mix the peaches, lemon juice, sugar, flour and salt. If using frozen, make sure peaches are thoroughly thawed before combining with the dry ingredients. Pour into the prepared pie pan after blind baking. Dot the peach mixture with butter.

To form the top lattice on your piecrust, take out the reserved portion of piecrust and roll out on a floured surface. Cut ½-inch (1.3-cm)-long strips and weave over the pie to form a lattice pattern. Once the top of the pie is covered with the interwoven lattice strips, use your fingers to press the outer edges together and seal by dipping a fork in flour and working a pattern around the crust hanging over the outer rim of the pan (making sure to cut off any excess dough with a paring knife). Next, make your egg wash by whisking your egg in a small bowl with a teaspoon of cold water. Brush the egg wash across top of latticed pie until the entire surface is coated. Place your pie in the preheated oven and bake for 15 minutes. Lower the heat to 350°F (177°C) and continue to bake for about 45 minutes, or until golden brown.

A COCKTAIL PARTY

Cocktail parties seem to have gone out of style. I vote to bring them back! Perhaps I've watched one too many old movies set in 1950s New York with glamorous women, in full skirts and with tiny waists, sipping champagne cocktails. Needless to say, I'm watching those movies, in a pair of pajamas, solo on the sofa and perhaps that's where the inspiration comes from to get off the sofa, make an effort and be social. It doesn't hurt that I love finger food, especially when it's hot. I have a gluttonous habit of positioning myself by the kitchen door at any event serving hot hors d'oeuvres—so I can pluck the mini morsels from the passing trays before they all disappear.

I wanted to start this chapter with two special cocktails from two very special women. I love this picture of Catskill Provisions' Claire Marin (left) and Tay Tea's Nini Ordoubadi (right) for so many reasons. These two people personify the dream behind Many Kitchens by being utterly passionate about their products, as well as by supporting other local businesses as they grow their own. Nini is an old friend who has become one of our producers and Claire is a producer who now feels like an old friend.

MENU

Queen Neferteati Cocktail
by Tay Tea

Don't Worry Bee Happy Cocktail
by Catskill Provisions

Gruyère and Tarragon Gougères
by Jacqueline et Jerome

Mini Sausage Rolls
by British Baking Company

Sweet Potato, Green Onion and
Traditional Mini Latkes
by Linda's Gourmet Latkes

Honey Maple Chicken Meatballs
by Catskill Provisions

QUEEN NEFERTEATI COCKTAIL
by TAY TEA

Makes 1 or 2 drinks

Nini Ordoubadi's aromatic blended teas lend themselves perfectly to cocktails. I once infused an entire bottle of gin with her Muse tea for a party and the champagne cocktails I made with it were the star of the evening. Muse tea was inspired by Nini's great-aunt Noushafarin Saad, a celebrated bon vivant, poet and tea blender in her native Iran. She makes this exotic cocktail with her wonderful Neferteati blend made with black tea, pomegranate, vanilla, blackberry leaves and calendula petals. The pomegranate seeds make the drink sinful and decadent.

4 oz (118 ml) freshly pressed pomegranate juice

2 oz (60 ml) prepared black tea, chilled (Earl Grey or English Breakfast would work well)

2 oz (60 ml) gin

Pomegranate seeds, for garnish

Mix all the ingredients, except the pomegranate seeds, in a cocktail shaker and pour over ice. Garnish with the pomegranate seeds. You absolutely can multiply this recipe in a pitcher: Just add the ice to the glasses before serving (do not place in the pitcher).

DON'T WORRY
BEE HAPPY COCKTAIL
by CATSKILL PROVISIONS

Makes 1 or 2 drinks

2 oz (60 ml) rye whiskey

1 oz (30 ml) St. Germain elderflower liqueur

2 tbsp (30 ml) freshly squeezed lemon juice

½ tsp honey

Dash of pure maple syrup

Lemon zest, for garnish

One of the guiding philosophies behind Catskill Provisions is to bring business to areas of New York State that really need it. Every stage of every product, from the growing of the wheat to the jarring of the honey, is all done in New York State. Claire Marin epitomizes the local food movement. She makes this cocktail with her extraordinary honey-infused rye whiskey. I've added ½ teaspoon of honey to the recipe in case you can't find her blend. Of course, I used Claire's raw wildflower honey and her NY state grade A maple syrup in this recipe, both of which I'm never without. Her whiskey is the latest addition to her expanding company that was born from a cathartic beekeeping hobby while she was working as a successful publishing executive.

Mix all the ingredients, except the lemon zest, in a cocktail shaker and serve in an up-glass or over ice. Garnish with the lemon zest. As with the Queen Neferteati Cocktail, you can multiply the amounts and serve from a large pitcher.

GRUYÈRE AND TARRAGON GOUGÈRES

by JACQUELINE ET JEROME

Makes 30 to 40 gougères

I felt like a baking pro (not a regular occurrence) when these came out of the oven. Golden brown on the outside with a light airy texture on the inside and just a hint of tarragon to complement the Gruyère, they burst in your mouth with the small bubbles amid pockets of warm cheesy bread. It's impossible to stop at one.

Preheat the oven to 390°F (199°C) and measure your ingredients so they are ready to add easily once you begin. In a medium-size saucepan, bring the 1 cup (240 ml) of water and the butter to a boil. Lower the heat to a simmer and add the flour all at once. Stir rapidly with a wooden spoon, then let it dry for a minute. Remove the pan from the heat and let cool for about 5 minutes (so when you add the eggs, they won't cook). Add the eggs, one at a time, stirring after each addition. Stir in the Gruyère, tarragon, salt, nutmeg and black pepper to taste.

Lay parchment paper on two baking sheets. Spoon out small balls of dough onto your baking sheets, with at least an inch (2.5 cm) separating the spoonfuls. Since the mixture is slightly sticky, a good way to make this easy on yourself is to use a melon baller or a tablespoon and wet it with water between scoops. This will give you a nice round top and will stop your hands from getting covered with dough.

Place your baking sheets in the center of the oven and bake for 25 minutes. As the balls bake, they will puff slightly and the tops will color a wonderful shade of golden brown. Remove from the oven and let cool for a minute before serving.

1 cup (240 ml) water

4½ tbsp (80 g) unsalted butter, diced

5 oz (150 g) all-purpose flour

4 large eggs

5 oz (150 g) Gruyère cheese, grated

2 tbsp (5 g) roughly chopped fresh tarragon leaves

½ tsp salt

¼ tsp freshly grated nutmeg

Freshly ground black pepper

MINI SAUSAGE ROLLS
by BRITISH BAKING COMPANY

Makes about 30 mini sausage rolls

1 lb (450 g) homemade or
store-bought all-butter
puff pastry

2 large eggs

1 lb (450 g) pork sausage meat
(I like to use English bangers)

2 tbsp (5 g) fresh sage, chopped

½ tsp chipotle chile powder

½ cup (30 g) bread crumbs or
panko

Salt and freshly ground
black pepper

Poppy seeds (optional)

You're never far from a sausage roll in England and I have a terrible weakness for them. Fortunately (or unfortunately), there is an English store, Myers of Keswick, just blocks from me in the West Village, which makes a good one, but it's Wendy's, of British Baking Company, that really reminds me of home. It must be the sage and chile she mixes into the sausage meat before wrapping them in an all-butter puff pastry and baking. They are impossible to eat without covering yourself in crumbs and getting your hands greasy. Most sausage rolls are best devoured in private, but mini sausage rolls like these can be nibbled in (almost) ladylike fashion and are more commonly found at children's parties than at cocktail parties. I love them so much I wanted to include them here. Consider them a (slightly) more sophisticated version of pigs in a blanket.

Preheat the oven to 400°F (204°C).

If you're using store-bought puff pastry, defrost in the fridge—you don't want it too soft. Divide the pastry into four portions and roll each as thinly as possible into 10 x 4-inch (25.5 x 10-cm) rectangles—remember they will puff up when baked. Beat the eggs with 2 teaspoons (10 ml) of water. Brush one long edge of each pastry rectangle with the egg wash.

In a large bowl, mix the sausage meat with the chopped sage, chipotle powder, bread crumbs, salt and pepper. Roll the meat into a long rope about ¾-inch (2-cm) in diameter—thinner or fatter as you prefer. Divide into four portions and set one lengthwise in the middle of each pastry rectangle. Starting from the egg-free long edge, roll the pastry over the meat, pressing on the egg-washed edge to seal. If using poppy seeds, sprinkle some over the sausage rolls.

Line a baking sheet with parchment paper and set the sausage rolls down about ½-inch (1.3-cm) apart. Brush the rolls with the egg wash and bake for 20 to 25 minutes, until nicely browned all over. Slice into bite–sized pieces, about 1 inch (2.5 cm). You can make them ahead of time, but do reheat them before serving as they're so much better straight from the oven.

SWEET POTATO, GREEN ONION AND TRADITIONAL MINI LATKES
by LINDA'S GOURMET LATKES

Makes around 45 bite-size latkes

Linda's latkes are easily the best I've ever had. She makes them in all sizes and all flavors. I've tried them all several times and I still can't decide which my favorite is. Get creative with the toppings for your cocktail party. Go Italian and use the Balsamic Fig and Goat Cheese Crostini (page 143) from our Italian Menu. Or add some leftover Mole Beef Tacos (page 131) from our Mexican Menu. Of course, if money is no object, by all means, top with a dollop of sour cream and caviar!

For a cocktail party, make a bunch, freeze and reheat in the oven, without thawing, just before serving.

Shred the potatoes and place in cold water; when ready to combine the ingredients, drain well, wringing out with your hands several times, until all the water is removed. Squeeze the grated onion as well, to remove any excess liquid and combine with the squeezed-dry potatoes, eggs, salt, pepper, flour and baking powder.

In a large skillet with at least 2-inch (5-cm) sides, heat the oil until bubbly. As your oil is heating, line a baking sheet with paper towels for your finished latkes. Test by frying a spoonful of the latke mixture first and when small bubbles form along the latke, your oil is ready to go. To fry the latkes, take a spoonful of your potato mixture and press it into a soft ball. The trick is to go thin to win. By placing them in the pan with a fork, the latkes come out crispy and fried on the outside and perfectly light and airy on the inside. For bite-sized latkes, the diameter should be 1½ to 2 inches (4 to 5 cm), for slightly larger ones, 2½ to 3 inches (6.5 to 7.5 cm). Make sure your oil isn't smoking at any point, as that is getting too hot. Work in batches to avoid overcrowding. Cook until the edges are crispy, about 2 minutes per side. When the latkes are finished, place on your paper towel–lined baking sheet to cool. Sprinkle with a little sea salt, add your desired topping and serve. If freezing, allow to cool completely first.

To serve reheated latkes, preheat your oven to 450°F (232°C). Place the latkes on a baking sheet and bake for 5 minutes, until they sizzle. Another cocktail tip is to warm them in batches so that each tray of latkes is nice and warm for your guests. You can replenish the trays throughout the party.

VARIATIONS: If you want to make different varieties of latkes, you can add green onion or sweet potato. For green onion latkes, add ½ cup (75 g) of chopped green onions to the mixture before frying. And for sweet potato latkes, add ½ cup (75 g) of shredded sweet potatoes to the mixture.

6 russet potatoes, peeled

1 small onion, grated (½ cup [75 g]) (see note)

3 large eggs

1 tsp sea salt, plus more for sprinkling

¼ tsp freshly ground black pepper

¼ cup (22 g) all-purpose flour

2 tsp (10 g) baking powder

1 tbsp (15 ml) vegetable or canola oil, plus more for frying

TOPPING SUGGESTIONS

Crème fraîche and smoked salmon with sprig of dill

Pomegranate seeds and Greek yogurt

Applesauce and ground cinnamon

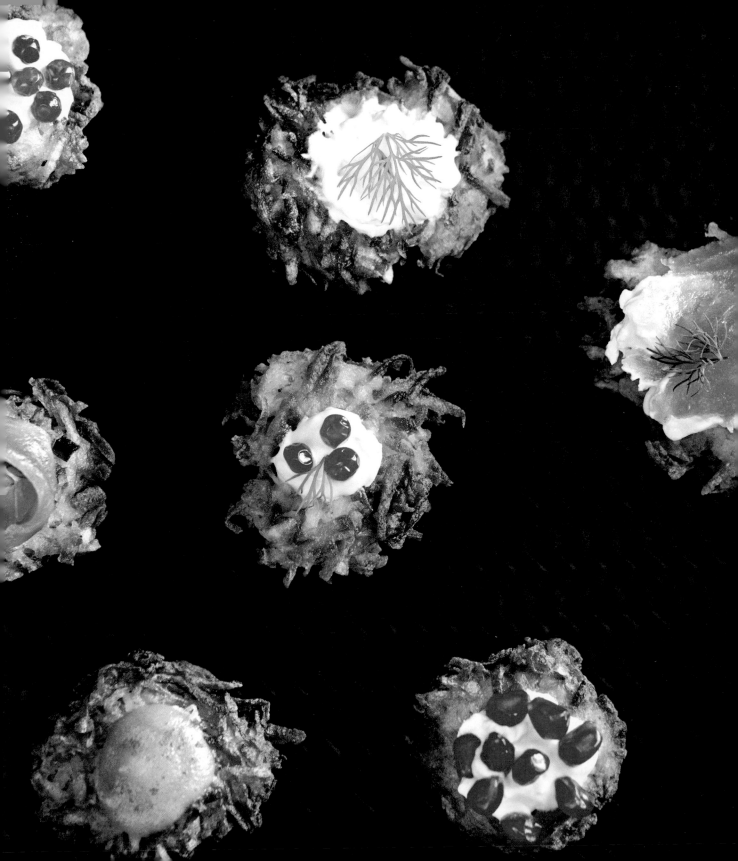

HONEY MAPLE CHICKEN MEATBALLS
by CATSKILL PROVISIONS

Serves 6

2 tsp (10 ml) light olive oil

1 onion, finely chopped

1 Granny Smith apple, peeled, cored and roughly chopped

2 chicken breasts, roughly chopped

1 tbsp (2.5 g) fresh parsley

1 tbsp (2.5 g) fresh thyme

1 chicken bouillon cube

1 cup (50 g) dried white bread crumbs

1 tsp ground ginger

1 tsp salt

1 tsp freshly ground black pepper

⅔ cup (50 g) all-purpose flour

GLAZE

2 tbsp (30 ml) honey

2 tbsp (30 ml) pure maple syrup

2 tbsp (30 ml) balsamic vinegar

Meatballs are a cocktail party staple and I love them all, from the Swedish meatballs of the 1970s to the lamb meatballs (page 118) I've included in the tapas menu. These chicken ones have been an excellent addition to my meatball repertoire. The finishing glaze adds a wonderful sweetness that makes them the irresistable party food.

Heat the olive oil in a pan and sauté half of the onion until really soft but not browned, about 5 minutes.

Put the apple, chicken, sautéed onion and remaining raw onion, herbs, bouillon cube, bread crumbs and ground ginger in a food processor and blitz until minced. Season with the salt and pepper.

Scoop out and make into about 20 little balls (about the size of a Ping-Pong ball), roll in the flour and fry in shallow vegetable oil in a skillet over low heat until lightly golden and cooked through, 2 to 4 minutes per side. Cook in batches so as not to overcrowd the pan and turn regularly so as not to burn the outside

MAKE THE GLAZE: In a small saucepan, bring the glaze ingredients to a boil and cook over medium heat until the sauce thickens, 5 to 10 minutes depending on the thickness of your balsamic vinegar. Add the glaze to the meatballs and shake the pan well until they are all fully coated.

A GERMAN DINNER

Schaller & Weber has been making outstanding sausages for over seventy-five years. Its store on the Upper East Side of Manhattan, open since 1937, is still largely unchanged, as are the techniques used to make its award-winning sausages and cured meats. Everything from the floor tiles and ceiling to the friendly expert butchers behind the counter makes me feel like I've not only walked into a different era but a different country, too. Founded by master butcher Ferdinand Schaller after he emigrated from Stuttgart to the United States in 1927, the business has stayed in the family ever since and is now run by Ferdinand's grandson, Jeremy Schaller. Their sausages are so good that they have repeatedly won gold medals in Germany, Holland and Austria.

I've loved working with Schaller & Weber since first discovering the firm at a beer hall in 2013. I was excited to put together this menu with Jeremy, using Schaller family classic recipes tweaked and updated by Alex, the chef of Schaller & Weber's newly opened café. I also wanted to make sure to include a recipe for mustard from Bryan Mitchener and Justin Hoffman of Mustard and Co., who make incredible small-batch mustards in Seattle. It turned out to be a wonderful hearty menu full of the flavors of Germany and perfect for a cold winter's night.

MENU

Braised Bratwurst with
Apples and Onions
by Schaller & Weber

Kaese Spaetzle with Bacon
by Schaller & Weber

Classic Stone-Ground
German Mustard
by Mustard and Co.

Kaiserschmarrn with
Vanilla Cream Sauce
by Schaller & Weber

BRAISED BRATWURST WITH APPLES AND ONIONS
by SCHALLER & WEBER

Serves 6 to 8

The pinnacle of the book publishing calendar is the Frankfurt Bookfair. Every October, 275,000 publishers from 100 countries take over the city for a week and grind it to a halt. Everyone is on expense accounts and away from home, so the drinks flow freely well into the wee hours, as deals are made and friends are reunited. I survived fifteen Frankfurt Bookfairs thanks to a diet of bratwurst and Coca-Cola. No matter how exhausted I was after each fair, I still miss the excitement. The first time I made this casserole, I was reminded of Frankfurt, but instead of eating a mediocre brat in a slightly soggy roll while standing up, I was able to fully enjoy bratwurst at their very best, mopped up with caramelized onions and apples as well as the killer Kaese Spaetzle (page 101).

Preheat the oven to 350°F (180°C)

In a large skillet, heat 2 tablespoons (29 g) of the butter. Add the onions and cook over medium heat for about 5 minutes. As they begin to soften, add the vinegar and maple syrup and turn up the heat. Cook for another 5 minutes, add the thyme, season with salt and pepper and transfer to a large baking dish.

Add another 2 tablespoons (29 g) of butter to the same skillet and add the apple slices. You want to brown these on both sides, about 10 minutes. Transfer these to the same baking dish, over the onions.

Add the remaining 2 tablespoons (29 g) of butter to the skillet, add the bratwurst and brown on all sides, about 10 minutes. Arrange these on top of the apples and onions. In the same skillet, bring the stock to a simmer, stir well, combining any good bits from the previous stages and pour over the bratwurst. Place the baking dish in the oven and bake for 45 minutes. Your home will be filled with the wonderful aromas of each stage of cooking from the sweetness of the onions and apples to the savoriness of the sausages.

Garnish with a few sprigs of fresh thyme and serve.

6 tbsp (86 g) unsalted butter

4 medium-size Vidalia onions, halved lengthwise and sliced

2 tbsp (30 ml) raw cider vinegar

¼ cup (60 ml) good-quality grade A maple syrup

3 tbsp (8 g) fresh thyme, plus 8 to 10 sprigs for garnish

Salt and freshly ground black pepper

2 Granny Smith apples, peeled, cored and sliced

10 links bratwurst

½ cup (118 ml) chicken stock

KAESE SPAETZLE WITH BACON
by SCHALLER & WEBER

Serves 6 to 8

1 lb (450 g) thick bacon,
cut into small dice

3 cups (270 g) all-purpose flour,
sifted

1½ tsp (7.5 g) salt

½ tsp freshly grated nutmeg

6 large eggs

1¼ cups (296 ml) heavy cream,
chilled

Unsalted butter, for baking dish

2 cups (240 g) grated Emmentaler
or other Swiss cheese

1 cup (120 g) grated Gruyère
cheese

1 large yellow onion, sliced
into ⅛" (3-mm) rings

1½ tbsp (4 g) fresh parsley,
finely chopped

Essentially German mac & cheese, this dish makes me want to move to the German Alps, become a ski bum and live in a mountain hut. Schaller & Weber sells frozen spaetzle, which is definitely easier than making your own, but not by as much as you would think. They also sell the most incredible double-smoked bacon that I have ever tasted. Their bacon or a high-quality equivalent, makes all the difference in the final flavor of the recipe.

Preheat the oven to 350°F (180°C).

In a skillet, render the bacon bits until browned and transfer to drain on paper towels. Reserve the bacon fat, as you will use it later.

In a large bowl, combine the sifted flour, salt and nutmeg and mix together with a fork. In a small bowl, beat the eggs until they turn light yellow, then whisk into the flour mixture. Continue to beat the batter while gradually adding the cream, until it comes together and becomes smooth and elastic. You may not need all the cream.

Heat a large pot of salted water to a boil, then lower the heat so it stays at a rolling boil. You will need to prepare an ice water bath and a buttered baking dish as well as have two slotted spoons ready.

Now comes the fun part! If you don't have a spaetzle maker (I certainly didn't), you can use a colander with large holes, or as I found to be easier, a large slotted spoon. You want the kind with holes rather than slits. Place a spoonful of batter on the slotted spoon. Using the back of another spoon, gently push the batter through the holes and into the boiling water below. As soon as they rise to the surface (about a minute), fish them out with the other slotted spoon, then shock them in the ice bath briefly before adding them to the buttered baking dish. Be careful not to let the spaetzle drop over the edges of the slotted spoon. I found it best to start with small amounts and work your way up as you get comfortable.

Add the bacon and cheese to the spaetzle and bake until the cheese melts and the spaetzle are slightly browned on top, 25 to 30 minutes. While the spaetzle are baking, heat the reserved bacon fat in the skillet until bubbling and fry the onion until crispy. Transfer to paper towels to drain and then sprinkle over the baked spaetzle along with the chopped parsley.

CLASSIC STONE-GROUND GERMAN MUSTARD
by MUSTARD AND CO.

Makes about 2 cups (500 g) mustard

Mustard & Co. was started in Seattle by two friends, Bryan Mitchener and Justin Hoffman. Their impetus? Why did such a simple condiment need to include so many additives? Now you can find out for yourself with this classic mustard. I really recommend trying some of their other varieties, too. Since working with Mustard and Co., my appreciation of mustard has been transformed for the better.

½ cup (85 g) brown mustard seeds

½ cup (85 g) yellow mustard seeds

⅓ cup (80 ml) balsamic vinegar

2 tsp (10 g) sea salt

⅓ cup (80 ml) extra-virgin olive oil

Crush the mustard seeds in a spice grinder. If you don't have one, I've found a food processor worked better than a blender. You want to have most of the seeds broken up. You could also use preground mustard seeds, but I liked the texture from grinding them yourself.

Combine all the ingredients, except the olive oil, plus ½ cup (118 ml) of water in a bowl, and using an immersion blender, blend together until the consistency is smooth.

Warning: Do not taste your mustard at this point in the process. No, seriously.

Slowly drizzle in the olive oil while continuing to whisk. Cover the bowl or transfer to a lidded container and refrigerate for 3 to 5 days. This allows the flavors to mature and your mustard to thicken. After your mustard has had a chance to hang out in your fridge for a few days, give it a good stir and have a taste. Make adjustments to your liking—if your mustard is too thick, add a small amount of water at a time and mix well. My batch needed a fair bit of water, so keep adding, a spoonful at a time and stirring until it reaches your desired consistency. Add salt to your preference.

KAISERSCHMARRN
WITH VANILLA CREAM SAUCE
by SCHALLER & WEBER

Serves 6 to 8

½ cup (75 g) raisins

7 large eggs, separated

1½ cups (135 g) all-purpose flour, sifted

¼ cup (48 g) granulated sugar

Pinch of salt

1½ cups (355 ml) cold milk

Unsalted butter, for baking dish

3 tbsp (24 g) confectioners' sugar, plus more for dusting

VANILLA CREAM SAUCE

1 cup (15 g) cream cheese, softened

1 cup (15 ml) heavy cream

2 tbsp (30 ml) freshly squeezed lemon juice

Seeds scraped from 1 vanilla bean

1 tsp honey

Kaiserschmarrn is named after the Emperor (Kaiser) Franz Joseph I of Austria who purportedly loved this shredded pancake dish. The vanilla sauce is usually made with Quark cheese, which can be difficult to find, so I've substituted cream cheese. Feel free to add berries, but I would really recommend trying this unique vanilla sauce alone. It's both savory and sweet and works perfectly with the pancakes.

Soak the raisins overnight, strain and set aside.

Preheat the oven to 350°F (180°C).

In a large bowl, beat the egg whites until soft peaks form. In a separate large bowl, mix together the sifted flour, granulated sugar and salt, using a fork. Add the egg yolks and milk to the flour mixture and beat until you get a smooth batter. Fold in the beaten egg whites and then the raisins. Let rest for 7 minutes.

Preheat a large, seasoned cast-iron skillet and pour in the batter. Cook until the underside of the pancake starts to turn golden brown, 3 to 5 minutes. At this point, it's pretty unwieldy to flip, so you can flip half at a time or even quarters, as it will be shredded later. Once turned, cook for another couple of minutes, turn off the heat and start ripping the pancake into bite-size pieces.

Butter a large baking dish and add the torn pieces of pancake. Sprinkle with the confectioners' sugar, place in the oven and bake for about 5 minutes, or until fully cooked through and the sugar has caramelized.

Dust with more confectioners' sugar and serve drizzled with the vanilla cream sauce.

MAKE THE VANILLA CREAM SAUCE: Mix together all the ingredients until you get a smooth sauce—40 seconds in the microwave on high speeds up the process!

SPANISH TAPAS

The options to include in a tapas menu are innumerable and who better to ask for a selection than Victoria Amory, whose philosophy is "effortless everyday entertaining." Not only is it a menu of all my top hits, but it's also the food that she grew up on in Spain and the food she now feeds her children in America. Entertaining is in Victoria's blood, not just as a Spaniard but as a child of the Count and Countess de la Maza, whose homes were always full of family, friends and food. She couldn't have been more patient or helpful with all my questions when testing the recipes, and as a result, we have created a tapas feast that made me want to not only hop on the subway to visit La Vara, but also to hop on a plane and visit Spain.

On Clinton Street in Brooklyn, La Vara has the best tapas I've ever had. Whenever I go, I want to order one of everything on the menu. Go with a group so you can sample multiple dishes. My advice is to make sure you get plenty of the croquetas, as I have almost come to blows over the last one. As my favorite part of any tapas meal, there was no doubt that croquetas had to be on this menu. Learning how to make them myself, although hazardous to my arteries, has been one of the most rewarding experiences of writing this book.

MENU

White Peach Sangria
by Many Kitchens

Tortilla de Patatas
with Hot Pink Mayonnaise
by Victoria Amory

Patatas Bravas with
Red Piri Piri Sauce
and Harissa Aioli
by Victoria Amory

Serrano Ham Croquetas
with Pimentón Aioli
by Victoria Amory

Lamb Meatballs
with Mint and Yogurt
by Victoria Amory

WHITE PEACH SANGRIA
by MANY KITCHENS

Serves 8 to 10

My godmother and her husband, Roly, used to throw a big party, known as Frutti di Mare, every Labor Day in Cape Cod. Roly made enormous vats of his two famous fish soups, one white and one red. Over a hundred people would line up, having brought their own bowls and spoons to get a taste of each. Much debate was had on which you started with, but there was never any debate as to how good they were poured over bruschetta slathered with rouille. All was washed down with equally enormous pitchers of sangria, both red and white. When I called Roly for the recipe for his white sangria, his first words were, "Take five gallons of wine!" I've reduced the quantities to a slightly more manageable size but it has lost none of its appeal.

FOR THE SIMPLE SYRUP: In a small saucepan, bring 1 cup (237 ml) of water and the sugar to a boil and let simmer until the sugar is dissolved, about 3 minutes. Remove from the heat and let cool completely.

FOR THE COCKTAIL: Mix all the ingredients in a pitcher, add the rum and simple syrup to taste and pour over ice. It's great to make this the day before, so the fruit takes in all the alcohol.

SIMPLE SYRUP

1 cup (237 ml) water

1 cup (190 g) granulated sugar

COCKTAIL

2 (750 ml) bottles dry white wine (sauvignon blanc or pinot grigio works well)

2 peaches, peeled and sliced (frozen peach slices work well, too)

1 orange, sliced lengthwise and then each half quartered (keep peels on)

2-4 oz (60-120 ml) dark rum

Simple Syrup, to taste

TORTILLA DE PATATAS WITH HOT PINK MAYONNAISE
by VICTORIA AMORY

Serves 6 to 8

- 6 tbsp (90 ml) extra-virgin olive oil
- 3 large potatoes, peeled and diced into ¼" (6-mm) cubes (see note)
- Salt
- ½ medium-size onion, diced
- 6 large eggs

According to Victoria, these potato tortillas, an everyday dish in Spanish households, spark endless controversy over everything from the proportion of eggs to potatoes, to whether you should add milk. Some like it runny; some, dry. Thank goodness, Victoria likes it just the way I do and has perfected her version over years of making it for her children and friends. Adults get the bonus of the latest addition to her growing condiment collection and her new favorite sauce, hot pink mayonnaise. I'm so excited that she's shared it with us here.

In a 9-inch (23-cm) nonstick omelet pan, heat 4 tablespoons (60 ml) of the olive oil over medium-high heat. Add the diced potatoes and season generously with salt. Stir the potatoes so they coat with the oil, lower the heat to low and cover with a lid. Cook, stirring regularly, until the potatoes are not quite fork-tender, 15 to 20 minutes. Stir in the onion and cook, uncovered, until the onion becomes translucent, 10 to 15 minutes.

In a large bowl, beat the eggs with a fork, add the potato mixture to the egg and stir to mix well. Clean the pan and return to the heat, add the remaining 2 tablespoons (30 ml) of olive oil and heat until hot. Add the potato mixture back to the pan and cook until the edges begin to brown, shaking the pan regularly. Cover with a flat lid or a large plate, flip over and slide back into the pan. It will not flip until the bottom has become nicely browned all over and formed a crust. Once flipped, keep over medium heat for a few more minutes, until the tortilla is cooked through and slides easily from the pan.

Serve hot or cold with a dollop of hot pink mayonnaise.

NOTE: While you prep them, place the potatoes in a salted water bath so they don't discolor. Dry them with a kitchen towel before adding them to the oil.

(continued)

HOT PINK MAYONNAISE (CONTINUED)

In a blender or food processor, purée together the egg, jalapeño, tomato paste, lemon juice and chili powder until very smooth. Slowly, in a stream, add the olive oil until the mayonnaise is thick. Add the salt to taste and adjust the seasonings.

Chill until ready to serve.

1 large egg

2 tbsp (64 g) red jalapeño peppers, finely diced (seeded or not, depending on how much heat you like)

1 tsp tomato paste

1 tbsp (15 ml) freshly squeezed lemon juice

¼ tsp chili powder, or more or less to taste

1 cup (237 ml) olive oil (not extra-virgin as it has too strong a flavor)

Salt

PATATAS BRAVAS WITH RED PIRI PIRI SAUCE AND HARISSA AIOLI

by VICTORIA AMORY

Serves 6

This recipe is Victoria's favorite version of this classic tapas dish. Roughly cut into rounds, parboiled and roasted, the potatoes are the perfect vehicle for the two sauces: Red Piri Piri and harissa aioli. Sometimes the potatoes are cubed and eaten with a toothpick; other times, they are cut into wedges. This dish should be made just before serving, as you want them piping hot. Alternate dipping the potato into each sauce.

Preheat the oven to 400°F (204°C).

Bring a large pot of salted water to a boil. Add the potato rounds and the bay leaf and cook until the potatoes are just soft, about 10 minutes. Using a slotted spoon, remove the potatoes from the water and place them in one layer on a cookie sheet lined with parchment paper. Drizzle with the olive oil and season with salt and pepper. Roast until golden, 15 to 20 minutes. Sprinkle with sea salt.

TO SERVE: In a large shallow platter, place each sauce in a ramekin and arrange the potatoes around them. Top with chopped parsley and use toothpicks or decorative mini-forks to dip the potatoes into the sauces. Alternatively, drizzle both sauces directly onto the potatoes.

(continued)

2 lb (907 g) fingerling potatoes, sliced into ¼" (6 mm) rounds

1 bay leaf

4 tbsp (60 ml) olive oil

Salt and freshly ground black pepper

Sea salt, for sprinkling cooked potatoes

1 cup (237 ml) Red Piri Piri Sauce (page 114)

1 cup (237 ml) harissa aioli (page 114)

Chopped fresh parsley, for garnish

RED PIRI PIRI SAUCE

Makes 1 cup (240 ml)

Piri Piri is a sauce prevalent in Portuguese and South African cuisines. Spicy and peppery, it is perfect to add flavor to chicken, eggs and fish, as well as these patatas.

In a food processor, combine all the ingredients, adding sea salt to taste and mix on high speed until smooth. It will last for about 1 week in the refrigerator.

BASIC AIOLI

Makes 1 cup (240 ml)

Aioli is a thick mayonnaise made using only egg yolks, garlic and olive oil. Victoria's recipe is absolutely foolproof and my new favorite sauce. Here we've given to the basic recipe; just add your favorite spice at the end and give it another whizz in the blender. The possibilities are endless, but in this book, we've used it with harissa for the Patatas Bravas (page 113), with pimentón for the Serrano Ham Croquetas (page 117) and with chipotle for the Yuca Fries (page 132). Have fun experimenting with different flavors.

In a blender, mix together the egg yolks, mashed garlic and lemon juice. Slowly, pour in the olive oil in a thin stream and continue to blend until all is emulsified and thick.

Start with a teaspoon of your chosen spice and increase until you've got the flavor you like. Taste to adjust the seasonings and refrigerate until ready to serve.

RED PIRI PIRI SAUCE

4 red and orange chile peppers, stemmed and seeded

1 medium-size red bell pepper, stemmed and seeded

1½ tsp (6 g) light brown sugar

1½ tsp (7 g) peeled and roughly chopped fresh ginger

1 garlic clove

⅓ cup (80 ml) extra-virgin olive oil

1 tbsp (15 ml) champagne vinegar

Sea salt

BASIC AIOLI

2 large egg yolks

1 garlic clove, mashed

1 tbsp (15 ml) freshly squeezed lemon juice

½ cup (118 ml) olive oil

1 tsp of your chosen spice, be it harissa, pimentón (smoked Spanish paprika) or chipotle

Salt

Spanish

SERRANO HAM CROQUETAS WITH PIMENTÓN AIOLI
by VICTORIA AMORY

Makes 30 to 40 croquetas

8 tbsp (115 g) unsalted butter

1 medium-size onion, very finely chopped

1 cup (90 g) all-purpose flour, plus more for dusting

3 cups (710 ml) whole milk

Freshly ground black pepper

Pinch of freshly grated nutmeg

4 oz (113 g) jamón serrano or prosciutto, diced

2 large eggs

1 cup (60 g) fine bread crumbs

Sunflower or mild olive oil, for frying

Pimentón aioli (page 114), for serving

When I go to Spain, I'm faced with the quandary of wondering how many croquetas I can eat without embarrassing myself. Luckily, I'm usually with my friend Geraldine who has lived there for 30 years and will let me devour as many as I'm physically able to, without any judgment. As I've proven time and time again while writing this book, they are by no means beyond the home cook's reach. Deliciously crispy on the outside and velvety soft on the inside, they are a must at every tapas feast.

Croquetas freeze beautifully, so make a double batch and keep them in your freezer. Cook them frozen, without thawing.

In a saucepan, heat the butter over medium heat and sauté the onion until translucent and soft. Add the flour and stir to make a thick sauce and "toast" the flour. Add the milk slowly, whisking as you go. Add the pepper and nutmeg and continue to whisk for 5 to 10 minutes, until you've made a thick, sticky béchamel sauce. Stir in the ham.

Spread the béchamel to a 1-inch (2.5-cm) thickness on a flat surface, such as a cookie sheet or a kitchen counter and let it cool completely. This helps form the croquetas better. Dust a separate flat work surface with a bit of flour, and using a spoon or a large melon baller, form the croquetas on the dusted surface into 2- to 2½-inch (5- to 6.5-cm) cylinders, like the shape of your thumb.

In a bowl, whisk the eggs. Place the bread crumbs in another bowl. Dip the croquetas in the eggs and then coat them with bread crumbs to completely cover them. In a large sauté pan, heat about ½ inch (1.3 cm) of oil over medium heat (you know it's ready if the oil bubbles when you add the croquetas) and begin to fry the croquetas in small batches until golden on all sides, about 2 minutes per side. Add more oil as needed and drain the pan if the bread crumbs begin to burn. Transfer the croquetas to absorbent paper towels and serve hot with the pimentón aioli

LAMB MEATBALLS
WITH MINT AND YOGURT
by VICTORIA AMORY

Makes about 30 meatballs

These incredibly juicy lamb meatballs can be a meal unto themselves. Victoria used to eat them as a child, with piles of crispy potatoes and mountains of peas. Here they are the centerpiece of this largely meatless tapas feast, with the mint and yogurt hinting at the Moorish influence in Spanish cooking.

In a large bowl, mix together the lamb, mint, bread crumbs, egg, salt and pepper. Form into 1-inch (2.5-cm) balls.

In a large sauté pan, heat the olive oil over high heat until smoking. Cook the meatballs until golden on all sides but not cooked through, about 2 minutes per side. You will need to work in batches. Using a slotted spoon, transfer each batch to paper towels.

Discard all but 2 tablespoons (30 ml) of the oil left in the pan. Add the sherry, bring to a boil and reduce to a thick syrup. Return the meatballs to the pan, coating them with the pan juices. Add the tomato sauce and simmer over low heat until the meatballs are cooked through and the sauce is bubbly, about 15 minutes. Garnish with additional fresh mint and a dollop of Greek yogurt.

2 lb (907 g) ground lamb

½ cup (20 g) fresh mint, finely chopped, plus extra for serving

2 tbsp (7 g) bread crumbs

1 large egg

Sea salt and freshly ground black pepper

4 tbsp (60 ml) olive oil

½ cup (118 ml) cooking sherry

2 cups (322 g) Fresh Marinara Sauce (page 147)

Greek yogurt, for serving

A MEXICAN FIESTA

I first visited Mexico in 1992 while backpacking through Central America with a friend before heading off to university. Our journey started in Mexico City and ended a couple of months later in Tulum. Back then, Tulum was not the hipster destination it has become today. In 1992, there were a couple of places where we could hang our hammock a stone's throw from the majestic Mayan ruins. By that point in our trip, we had picked up a group of seven friends traveling together and I remember our final night on the beach with nine hammocks interlocking in a circular hut.

That summer was the beginning of a lifelong love affair with Mexico. For the last few years, I've been returning to Tulum every January to eat my weight in tacos washed down with margaritas. I love returning every year to the same little hotel on the beach where everyone's in bed before ten p.m. and up with the sun. I make the obligatory pilgrimages to the foodie meccas, most notably The Hartwood, but I'm happiest staying at the hotel for a quiet, unassuming meal. The menu I've put together here includes all my favorite Mexican flavors plus a recipe for tacos that are as delicious as any I've had in Mexico.

MENU

Watermelon Cilantro Margarita
by Many Kitchens

Sopa Tarasca
by Rancho Gordo

Mole Colorado
by Bunches and Bunches

Mole Beef Tacos
by Bunches and Bunches

Yuca Fries with Chipotle Aioli
by Victoria Amory

Churros with Vanilla
Caramel Sauce
by the Caramel Jar

WATERMELON CILANTRO MARGARITA
by MANY KITCHENS

Makes 1 drink

Watermelon makes this margarita so amazingly thirst-quenching that you have to be careful not to guzzle it down too quickly. I've had to ask Lana, who prepares it so expertly at my local bar, to cut me off after a couple or I'm liable to convince myself that I missed my calling as a professional salsa dancer.

FOR THE SIMPLE SYRUP: In a small saucepan, bring 1 cup (237 ml) of water and the sugar to a boil and let simmer until the sugar is dissolved, about 3 minutes. Remove from the heat and let cool completely.

FOR THE COCKTAIL: In the glass of a cocktail shaker, muddle the lime half and cilantro with the simple syrup.

If you want to have a salt rim, take two saucers and fill the first with simple syrup and the second with kosher salt. Dip the rim of a rocks glass first in the simple syrup and then into the salt.

To complete the cocktail, add the tequila, Cointreau and watermelon juice to the shaker. Add ice cubes and shake vigorously. Strain into the rimmed rocks glass or a mason jar filled with ice. Complete with a watermelon cube or lime wedge.

SIMPLE SYRUP

1 cup (237 ml) water

1 cup (190 g) granulated sugar

COCKTAIL

½ lime, plus 1 wedge for garnish (optional)

3 sprigs cilantro, torn by hand

½ oz (15 ml) simple syrup, plus more for salt rim (optional)

Coarse kosher salt (optional)

2 oz (60 ml) silver or platinum/blanco tequila

1 oz (30 ml) Cointreau

1½ oz (44 ml) freshly squeezed watermelon juice

1 watermelon cube or slice, for garnish (optional)

SOPA TARASCA
by RANCHO GORDO

Serves 4 to 6

3 tbsp (45 ml) extra-virgin olive oil

½ white onion, thinly sliced

2 garlic cloves, minced

1 lb (450 g) plum tomatoes, chopped

4 cups (804 g) cooked Mayocoba, Yellow Indian Woman or Alubia Blanca beans, in their broth

3 cups (710 ml) chicken or vegetable stock

1 tsp dried Indio or Mexican oregano

Salt

Corn, safflower or peanut oil, for frying

2 day-old corn tortillas, cut into thin strips

2 ancho chiles, seeded and cut into narrow strips

½ cup (60 g) queso fresco or other mild, wet white cheese

Fresh cilantro leaves, for serving

This adapted version of a local soup from Michoacan, Mexico, is tailor-made for bean lovers. Traditionally you would use Bayo beans, which are a very mild legume. Using heirlooms kicks up the textures and flavors; experiment with what you have on hand.

Rancho Gordo's Steve Sando told me he loves to place the soup bowls on the table with cheese and tortilla strips, and once everyone is seated, dramatically swoosh in and ladle the hot soup over the cheese and strips from a soup tureen.

Heat the olive oil over medium heat in a heavy skillet. Add the onion, garlic and tomatoes and sauté until soft, about 10 minutes. Remove from the heat and let cool slightly. Transfer to a blender and mix until smooth. Transfer to a stock, food processor or soup pot.

Purée the beans and their broth in the blender, adding some of the chicken stock if necessary to keep the blades moving. Add them to the pot. Bring to a simmer and cook, stirring occasionally, for about 5 minutes.

Add the chicken stock and oregano and season with salt. Cook for 10 minutes or so.

Meanwhile, pour the oil into a small, heavy skillet to a depth of about ½ inch (1.3 cm). Heat over medium-high heat until it is shimmering. Fry the tortilla strips, turning with tongs, until crisp and medium brown, 2 to 3 minutes. Transfer to paper towels to drain. Fry the ancho chile strips until they puff up and emit a spicy aroma, 2 to 3 seconds. Remove quickly, as they can become bitter if overcooked.

In warmed bowls, put some cheese, fried tortilla strips and fried ancho chile. Pour in the hot soup. Garnish with cilantro and queso fresco.

(continued)

STEVE SANDO ON HOW TO COOK BEANS

Sauté half a chopped onion in about 1 tablespoon (15 ml) of fat (oil, lard, bacon fat, etc.). Place in a slow cooker along with any other aromatics you'd like (such as Mexican oregano, garlic or bay leaf), followed by beans that have been picked over and rinsed. Cover with water (about one part beans to three or four parts water). Set the heat to high and give the contents a stir. Do this in the morning, and your beans should be done by the afternoon. The cooking time will be 4 to 6 hours, depending on your slow cooker and the variety of beans.

A FEW EXTRA TIPS

You can expect 1 cup (about 200 g) of dried beans to yield about 3 cups (about 600 grams) of cooked beans. One pound (455 g, or about 2 cups) of dried beans will yield about 6 cups (about 1.2 kg) of cooked beans.

We discussed the benefits of soaking on page 50. Basically, the only thing it will do is speed up the cooking time and can help the beans to cook more evenly, so if you have the time to do it, it won't hurt. Steve doesn't recommend soaking for more than six hours, or the beans may begin to sprout.

Many believe that adding salt (or acids, such as tomatoes or vinegar) too early in the cooking process prevents the beans from getting soft. Steve has found this especially true with older beans.

You can store leftover cooked beans in the refrigerator for up to five days and you can freeze them as well. If you are storing beans in the refrigerator, keep them in their cooking liquid so they don't dry out.

MOLE COLORADO
by BUNCHES AND BUNCHES

Makes more than 1 quart (945 ml) mole; serves 10 to 12

3 tbsp (30 g) sesame seeds

1 tbsp (10 g) cumin seeds

2 tsp (4 g) coriander seeds

2 whole cloves

3 allspice berries

1 (1½" [4-cm]) cinnamon stick

5 tbsp (74 ml) vegetable oil

6 dried pasilla negro chiles, stemmed and seeded

2 dried New Mexico or guajillo chiles, stemmed and seeded

2 dried ancho chiles, stemmed and seeded

3 dried pasilla de Oaxaca or dried chipotle chiles, stemmed and seeded

3 tbsp (28 g) raisins

½ cup (85 g) almonds, roughly chopped

¼ cup (40 g) raw pumpkin seeds

2 corn tortillas, quartered

2 medium-size plum tomatoes

5 tomatillos

I couldn't have been more excited when Tamalpais, of Bunches and Bunches, offered to create a new mole sauce especially for this book. Pai, as she's known, produces three mole sauces, each as distinctive and complex as any I've tasted. This new sauce is an ode to her first tastes of moles, as a child visiting Tijuana. It's worth mentioning that it's named "Colorado" for its colorful palette as opposed to the U.S. state, as I mistakenly thought! I love the way she described it to me as a "gateway" mole to the vast and rich world of Mexican cuisine.

Making a large batch is well worthwhile, as it is a labor of love and will spice up pretty much anything from a grilled pork chop to a soft poached egg. The sauce will keep in the refrigerator for up to two weeks and freezes wonderfully.

In a dry skillet, combine the sesame seeds with the cumin, coriander, cloves, allspice and cinnamon stick. Toast over moderately low heat, stirring, until fragrant, about 2 minutes. Transfer to a spice grinder and let cool completely. Grind the mixture to a fine powder. In the same skillet, add 2 tablespoons (30 ml) of the oil. Toast the dried chiles until fragrant. Transfer to a large bowl. In the same skillet, add 1 tablespoon (15 ml) of the oil. Stir in the raisins, almonds, pumpkin seeds and tortillas. Cook the mixture over moderately low heat until the almonds are toasted and the raisins are plump, 5 to 7 minutes. Transfer tortilla mixture to the bowl.

Add the tomatoes and tomatillos to the skillet and cook over medium-high heat, turning, until the skins are blistered and blackened on all sides, about 12 minutes. Transfer the blistered tomatoes and tomatillos to a bowl.

(continued)

MOLE COLORADO (continued)

In a heavy-bottomed pot or Dutch oven over medium heat, combine the remaining 2 tablespoons (30 ml) of oil and the onion and caramelize, about 15 minutes. Add the garlic, tomatoes and tomatillos. Stir in the toasted spices and thyme and cook over moderately high heat until fragrant, about 3 minutes. Add the chile mixture (scrape down the sides of the bowl to include all the oil). Add 5 cups (1.2 L) of water, bring to a boil, turn down the heat, cover partially and simmer for 1 hour. Remove from the heat. Add the chocolate, lime juice, cilantro (stems and all) and 1 tablespoon (15 g) of salt. Using an immersion blender (or working in batches in a stand blender), purée until smooth. Season the mole sauce with salt and pepper.

1 medium-size onion, diced

5 garlic cloves, peeled and crushed with the side of your chef's knife

1 tsp dried thyme

2 oz (55 g) dark chocolate, coarsely chopped

¼ cup (60 ml) freshly squeezed lime juice

½ bunch fresh cilantro, plus more for garnish

Salt and freshly ground black pepper

MOLE BEEF TACOS
by BUNCHES AND BUNCHES

Serves 6

MOLE BEEF

2 lb (907 g) organic beef chuck

Salt and freshly ground black pepper

Mole Colorado (page 127)

TO SERVE

12 small corn tortillas

1 avocado, cubed

Queso fresco, crumbled

4 radishes, sliced paper thin

Fresh cilantro leaves, for garnish

In the last few years, I've become slightly obsessed with tacos. My favorite are from Empellón Taqueria on West 4th Street in the West Village. Just writing about it makes me want to run over there for a plate of its skirt steak tacos on which I like to pour Empellón's famous smoked cashew salsa. Their tacos inspired me to start experimenting at home. This taco recipe rivals any I've had at Empellón and if you find yourself with any leftover mole beef (unlikely), it makes unbelievable nachos. Just fill a cast-iron pan or cookie sheet with tortilla chips, cover with your pulled mole beef and some shredded cheese and bake for ten minutes. Top with shredded jalapeños and sour cream.

Preheat the oven to 350°F (180°C).

Season the meat with salt and pepper. In a large Dutch oven, brown the meat on all sides over high heat, about 5 minutes per side. Cover with the mole sauce and bring to a simmer. Cover and braise in the oven until the meat is very tender, 2 to 3 hours.

TO SERVE: Just before you remove the meat from the oven, divide the tortillas in two stacks, wrap in foil and place in the oven. Transfer the meat to a chopping board or platter and shred with two forks. Return it to the pot and stir in the cooked sauce. I like to put the pot of beef in the middle of the table with the tortillas wrapped in a tea towel along with all the fixings and let everyone prepare their own tacos just the way they like them.

YUCA FRIES
WITH CHIPOTLE AIOLI
by VICTORIA AMORY

Makes 4 to 6 servings

A twist on your standard French fry, these don't require boiling before you fry and don't discolor once cut. The trick to the recipe is removing that hard, ominous skin, which is easily accomplished with a good knife. It does make me wonder who first discovered that yuca was a food. I suspect a food born more out of desert necessity, it now provides the basis for a great many recipes, all thanks to that first brave soul.

FOR THE AIOLI: In a blender, mix together the egg yolks, mashed garlic and lemon juice. Slowly, pour in the olive oil in a thin stream and continue to blend until all is emulsified and thick.

Start with a teaspoon of chipotle and increase until you've got the flavor you like. Taste to adjust the seasonings and refrigerate until ready to serve.

FOR THE YUCA FRIES: In a large saucepan or Dutch oven, heat the oil to 350°F (177°C). Remove all the tough outer skin from the yuca, using a sharp knife. Cut the yuca into ¼- x 4-inch (6-mm x 10-cm) strips. Add the yuca to the oil and fry until golden brown, 5 to 7 minutes. With a slotted spoon, remove the yuca from the oil and drain on paper towels.

Season the hot yuca fries with sea salt and lime zest and serve with chipotle aioli.

CHIPOTLE AIOLI

2 large egg yolks

1 garlic clove, mashed

1 tbsp (15 ml) freshly squeezed lemon juice

½ cup (118 ml) olive oil

1 tsp of chipotle

Salt

YUCA FRIES

3 cups (710 ml) canola oil

2 medium-size fresh yuca

Sea salt

Zest of 1 lime

CHURROS WITH VANILLA CARAMEL SAUCE
by THE CARAMEL JAR

Makes 12 (4" [10-cm]) churros

CINNAMON COATING

½ cup (96 g) granulated sugar

1 tsp ground cinnamon

CHURROS

About 5 cups (1 L) vegetable oil, for frying

1 tsp pure vanilla extract

1 tbsp (15 ml) honey

½ tsp salt

1½ tsp (4 g) ground cinnamon

3 tbsp (43 g) unsalted butter

1 cup (90 g) all-purpose flour

1 egg

Nicole Ebbitt started her caramel company in 2010, making individual hand-wrapped caramels that were the best I had ever tasted. She's expanded her line to include caramel corn, featured earlier in this book (page 77), as well as caramel sauces like this one. She is as fabulous and sweet as the food is.

Churros are another street-food favorite from Mexico that has found its way to New York. One that I thought far beyond my capabilities in the kitchen. An incredibly fun treat to serve at your fiesta that will seriously impress your friends, it's made even more delectable when dipped into Nicole's heavenly caramel sauce.

MAKE THE CINNAMON COATING: In a shallow dish, mix the cinnamon and sugar until blended.

PREPARE THE CHURROS: Heat the oil to 375° to 400°F (190° to 200°C).

Combine 1 cup (237 ml) of water and the vanilla, honey, salt, cinnamon and butter over medium-high heat. Bring to a boil. Remove from the heat and add the flour. Stir vigorously with a wooden spoon. Transfer to a bowl. Add the egg. Mix on low speed with an electric mixer until the flour mixture and egg are combined and form a sticky, thick batter.

Fill a piping bag with a star tip (the largest you can find) with batter, leaving 2 inches (5 cm) at the top to seal. Once your oil is hot, make a tester churro. To do so, squeeze out about an inch (2.5 cm) of batter into your oil and fry for about 1 minute, until golden brown. Make sure most of the air is out of your piping bag and pipe your churros. You can make them as long as you like, but about 4 inches (10 cm) long works nicely for a small bite. When you pipe the churros, hold your piping bag straight over the pot of oil and squeeze to release until you have your desired length. Cut the end with kitchen scissors and fry for 1 to 2 minutes, until golden brown. Repeat with the remaining batter. As you finish a churro, roll it in the cinnamon sugar coating, then drain on paper towels. Let cool and dip away in the delicious caramel sauce. These taste best if served immediately.

(continued)

VANILLA CARAMEL SAUCE (CONTINUED)

Makes 2 to 3 cups (475-700 ml)

Rub a saucepan with the melted butter (prevents sugar crystals from sticking to sides of pan), then combine ½ cup (118 ml) of water, the sugar and the syrup in the pan. Heat over medium-high heat until the sugar is dissolved. If any sugar crystals linger on the side of the pan, wipe down during the initial sugar-heating process. Bring the sugar mixture to a boil and cook until it reaches a warm amber color. The sugar will darken quickly, so be careful not to scorch it. Remove from the heat. *Very* gently (it will bubble ferociously, splatter and steam) add the butter, cream, vanilla and salt. Return the pan to medium-low heat. Cook until the caramel reaches 229°F (110°C). Remove from the heat and pour into a storage container. We love mason jars for this! Let cool and refrigerate. Best served warm.

If sugar crystals appear, heat again and then serve

5 tbsp (72 g) unsalted butter, plus 1 tsp, melted, for pan

1½ cups (290 g) granulated sugar

½ cup (118 ml) brown rice syrup or light corn syrup

1 cup (237 ml) heavy cream

1 tsp pure vanilla extract

1 tsp fleur de sel

AN ITALIAN SUPPER

Italian food is my first true love. It's what I was brought up on and what I feel most confident and comfortable cooking. I learned to cook it the old-fashioned way by watching my mother at work in her kitchen. I've never seen her follow a recipe; everything was created *all'occhio*, meaning nothing was measured, just estimated by sight. Her pastas are second to none and it took some serious self-control not to add more of my favorite recipes to this chapter, but that's for another time and another book.

This Italian supper is one that can mostly be made in advance and is ideal for eating "family style," whether you're eating on your lap, cramped around a table in a tiny New York apartment, or around a larger table, under a vine-covered pergola, as the sun sets over the Tuscan hills. The recipes are hard to mess up and don't need all your attention—always my favorite kind. I want to be enjoying that Campari cocktail with everyone else and not fussing over exact measurements and precise timings. Just remember that the better the ingredients, the better the flavor; everything else will fall into place.

MENU

The Many Kitchens
Campari Cocktail
by Many Kitchens

Balsamic Fig and
Goat Cheese Crostini
by Many Kitchens

Ricotta Gnocchi
by Many Kitchens

Fresh Marinara Sauce
by Jar Goods

Beef Braised in Barolo
by Many Kitchens

Green Beans with Shallots
and Toasted Hazelnuts
by Many Kitchens

Chocolate Salami
by Daily Chocolate

THE MANY KITCHENS
CAMPARI COCKTAIL

Makes 1 drink

Growing up, the first thing my mother did when we arrived at the beach in Italy each summer was order a Campari Soda. It was her ritual that signified the beginning of summer. In Italy, Campari Soda comes ready mixed in little glass bottles whose design is as iconic to me as an old-fashioned Coca-Cola bottle. I remember being allowed to taste it as a child and thinking it was the most disgustingly bitter thing ever. I grew up and luckily my tastes did, too. I've now taken on the tradition and my first night in Italy each summer, sitting on my favorite stone wall overlooking the vineyard, is accompanied by a Campari, albeit a slightly jazzed up version.

1 oz (30 ml) gin

2 oz (60 ml) Campari

¼ cup (60 ml) freshly squeezed orange juice

½ cup (118 ml) tonic water

1 orange slice

Combine the gin, Campari and orange juice in a shaker with ice. Shake well and pour into a glass. Top with the tonic water and garnish with the orange slice.

BALSAMIC FIG AND GOAT CHEESE CROSTINI
by MANY KITCHENS

Serves 6

1 baguette

1 small log goat cheese

Fresh figs, thinly sliced

Aged balsamic vinegar

Fresh thyme sprig, for garnish

These crostini combine my favorite blend of flavors and textures: Sweet and savory as well as crunchy and creamy. It's the opposites-attract concept. Try to find a really good aged balsamic vinegar, or you can boil down a younger balsamic in a small saucepan to get the same rich syrup, even if it won't have the richness of flavor that you get from aging.

Slice the baguette thinly, toast and lay out on a platter. Spread some goat cheese on each slice and top with a slice of fig. Drizzle with a little balsamic and garnish with a small sprig of thyme.

RICOTTA GNOCCHI
by MANY KITCHENS

Serves 6

My favorite gnocchi in New York City are made at a lovely Italian restaurant in the West Village called Barbuto. The story goes that its famed chef and owner, Jonathan Waxman, was once cooking for a wedding and realized he had forgotten to defrost the gnocchi. Out of desperation, he threw the frozen gnocchi into a hot skillet and created something so deliciously crispy on the outside yet fluffy on the inside that they've been on his menu ever since. The same approach works as perfectly with the even-more-cloudlike ricotta gnocchi as it does with its potato cousins. I've given options below for boiling and frying, you can decide which you prefer. Both are incredibly easy and fast!

The gnocchi go wonderfully with tomato sauce (recipe follows) but for an alternative, you can serve with fresh sage leaves, browned in butter, and a generous handful of grated fresh Parmesan cheese.

1 lb (450 g) good-quality fresh ricotta cheese

½ cup (45 g) all-purpose flour, plus more for rolling

1 large egg, lightly beaten

½ cup (90 g) freshly grated Parmesan cheese

1 tbsp (14 g) unsalted butter, softened

½ tsp salt

2 tbsp olive oil, for frying (optional)

Layer a plate with a few sheets of paper towels and lay the ricotta on top. Add a few more layers on top and push down to extract as much liquid as possible. Leave to rest for about 20 minutes.

In a large bowl, mix together all the ingredients, except the olive oil, with your hands and form into a large ball of dough. You may need a little extra flour but try not to, as the less flour, the lighter the gnocchi will be. Wrap the dough in plastic wrap and refrigerate for at least an hour or overnight.

When ready to make the gnocchi, lightly flour a surface as well as a sheet pan lined with parchment paper. Divide the dough into eight pieces. With lightly floured hands, roll each piece into a rope ½- to ¾-inch (1.3- to 2-cm) thick. Cut the rope into ¾-inch (2-cm) pieces and transfer to the sheet pan. Continue until all the gnocchi have been cut. If you want to press the back of a fork lightly on each gnoccho, you can but it doesn't do much more than make it look pretty.

TO BOIL: Bring a large pot of salted water to a boil and begin to drop in the gnocchi. As they rise to the top, give them another minute and then remove with a large slotted spoon, add to your sauce and serve immediately.

TO FRY: Cover the sheet pan with another layer of parchment paper and then plastic wrap. Freeze overnight. When ready to cook, heat a large skillet over high heat and pour in 2 tablespoons (30 ml) of olive oil. Add the gnocchi and brown on both sides. This only takes a couple of minutes. Transfer with a slotted spoon to your sauce and serve immediately.

FRESH MARINARA SAUCE
by JAR GOODS

Makes 4 cups (945 ml) sauce

7 medium-size fresh ripe tomatoes (see note)

¼ cup (59 ml) extra-virgin olive oil

¼ cup (38 g), white onion, finely chopped

2 fresh garlic cloves, thinly sliced

1 tsp salt

1 tsp granulated sugar

½ cup (20 g) fresh basil (keep on stems, for easy removal)

The perfect marinara is a pantry staple, but I had struggled to find any artisan who was making it just right. When Melissa of Jar Goods first wrote to me to ask if she could send me a jar of her Classic Red, I admit to being less than hopeful. I feel very strongly about tomato sauce and had spent years trying every sauce on the market and was yet to find one that I would consider selling, let alone eating. I could tell the minute I opened the jar that my search was over. Here, Melissa has kindly shared with us a fresh take on her Classic Red, using ripe summer tomatoes.

This recipe is all about perfect, sun-ripened tomatoes. You need those beautifully misshapen, summer tomatoes where you can smell the sweetness bursting through the skin. Tomato season winds down at the end of August, so I spend those last hot weeks doubling, tripling and then even quadrupling this recipe so I can have a freezer supply to last until tomato season begins again in July.

Cut a small X on the bottom of each tomato. Bring a large pot of water to a boil and drop tomatoes into the boiling water for 30 seconds. Remove the tomatoes and run them under cold water until cool enough to peel.

Peel the tomatoes, then quarter them. Remove the seeds and any hard core.

In a large saucepan, heat the olive oil over medium heat. Add the onion and sauté until translucent, about 5 minutes. Add the garlic and sauté for roughly 1 minute more, until fragrant and just cooked but not browned. Add the fresh tomatoes and allow the sauce to come to a slow boil. Season with the salt and sugar and then simmer for 10 minutes.

Using a potato masher (you can also use a wooden spoon, but the masher is easier), crush the tomatoes in the pan.

Add the basil. Simmer for an additional 10 minutes. Taste, then continue to cook until the tomatoes are slightly jammy. Do not cook for more than 25 minutes because you want to preserve that fresh taste.

Remove the basil before using. This sauce can be made in advance and freezes very well.

NOTE: My favorite tomatoes are a variety called Big Boy, but a good beefsteak or heirloom will work, too. If tomatoes are not in season, you can substitute 1 (28-oz [(794-g)]) can of Italian Marzano whole tomatoes.

BEEF BRAISED IN BAROLO
by MANY KITCHENS

Serves 6

This hearty dish is from Piedmont, the region in the north of Italy where my mother is from. The beef should be tender and succulent when sliced and served beneath the sauce enriched with all the flavors from the wine, herbs and vegetables. My mother served it, as I do, on a bed of creamy polenta to mop up that savory sauce. Obviously, it's traditionally made with a bottle of Barolo but I make it with a good Chianti and it's just as delicious (and much cheaper!).

Braised beef definitely takes some time and work, but when it's doing its thing in the oven, your home will fill with the most delicious aromas and you'll remember why you made the effort.

In a large container, combine the vegetables, cloves, peppercorns, herbs, meat, wine and brandy.

Cover and leave to marinate in the fridge for as long as you can, at least 2 hours.

Preheat the oven to 350°F (180°C).

Remove the meat from its marinade, dry well and bring to room temperature. In a large Dutch oven, melt the butter and oil over high heat and brown the meat on all sides. When browned, transfer to a platter.

Using a slotted spoon, add the vegetables and herbs from the marinade to the pot and scrape the bottom of the pan. Sauté for about 5 minutes, then return the meat to the pot and season well. Add the rest of the marinade and bring to a simmer.

Cover tightly, place in the oven and braise for at least 3 hours, basting every 30 minutes and turning the meat once or twice. Once the meat is fork-tender, move the pot from the oven to the stovetop. Transfer the meat to a chopping board and remove the bay leaves and rosemary. Using an immersion blender, puree the sauce about halfway so there are still plenty of vegetables. Over medium heat, reduce the sauce by about half.

Slice the meat and return and return it to the sauce to warm, then serve over a bed of creamy polenta.

2 celery stalks, roughly chopped

1 onion, roughly chopped

2 carrots, roughly chopped

1 garlic clove, roughly chopped

3 whole cloves

Small handful of peppercorns

2 bay leaves

1 sprig rosemary

2 lb (907 g) beef shoulder steak or chuck

1 (750 ml) bottle red wine

½ cup (118 ml) brandy

2 tbsp (30 g) unsalted butter

4 tbsp (60 ml) olive oil

Salt and freshly ground black pepper

Polenta, for serving

GREEN BEANS WITH SHALLOTS AND TOASTED HAZELNUTS

by MANY KITCHENS

Serves 6

2 tbsp (30 ml) extra-virgin olive oil

5 shallots, thinly sliced

1½ lb (680 g) green beans, trimmed

2 tbsp (30 g) unsalted butter

Salt

Handful of hazelnuts, crushed into small pieces and toasted in a dry skillet

Green beans are always my vegetable of choice as they go with absolutely everything from fish to meat. They were a staple in my house while I was growing up and are perfect on their own or dressed up, as they are here, with crunchy hazelnuts and sweet shallots.

Heat the olive oil in a skillet over medium heat. Add the shallots and stir regularly until they begin to brown, about 5 minutes. Remove with a slotted spoon and leave to rest on a plate lined with a paper towel.

Bring a large pot of water to a boil and cook (or steam) the green beans for 4 to 5 minutes. You want to make sure they still have a nice crunch to them but that you can bite through easily. Drain the beans and mix well with the butter and a good sprinkling of salt.

Arrange the beans on a platter and top with the shallots and hazelnuts.

CHOCOLATE SALAMI
by DAILY CHOCOLATE

Lest there be any confusion, this is not a chocolate-covered salami; it is merely shaped like a salami.

This recipe is the result of a collaboration with the immensely talented chocolatier Jennifer Roberts. On Valentine's Day (or as I like to call it, Valentina's Day), my mother would always make me torrone molle. A rich, buttery, no-bake chocolate dessert that is delectable no matter when or how you eat it. We have always struggled with its appearance, though. We tried different shapes, covering it with edible flowers, all to no avail, until I saw a picture in a magazine of a chocolate salami. I sent my mother's recipe to Jen, who adapted it as only she could and it is now even more delicious, as well as something you can't wait to bring to the table and slice in front of everyone.

In a large bowl, using an electric mixer on low speed, cream together the butter and granulated sugar until light and fluffy. Add the cocoa powder, a little at a time, until all is absorbed and the mixture is richly dark in color, resembling a brownie mix.

Slowly add the coconut oil until well mixed. If using vanilla, brandy or rum, add it now. Then mix in the nuts and crumbled cookies. Divide the chocolate batter in two. Take your first half and drop onto a long sheet of plastic wrap. Wrap completely in plastic wrap and roll into a nice, smooth, salami-size cylinder. Be sure to roll out any air bubbles before sealing. Take the two ends of your plastic wrap and twist as you would a candy wrapper to seal. Repeat with your second half of the mixture. Refrigerate for at least 4 hours, or better yet, overnight to set completely.

Once your logs have chilled and set, you can begin to decorate them. Lay them on a sheet of waxed paper and dust generously with confectioners' sugar. Rub in the sugar so that it starts to take on the appearance of aged salami, not completely uniform but lighter white in spots; in others, more rubbed in. Dust with the sugar as much as necessary and be sure, if your hands are heating the chocolate too much, to work in a cool area or refrigerate again as needed. You can even add loops of trussing string along your chocolate salami to complete the look.

These salamis make wonderful gifts, but be sure to serve in a cool area. When ready to serve, remove the string and slice.

6 oz (70 g) unsalted butter, at room temperature

8 oz (227 g) granulated sugar

4 oz (113 g) good-quality organic, undutched, unsweetened cocoa powder

3 oz (35 g) coconut oil, melted

2 tbsp (30 ml) pure vanilla extract, brandy or rum (optional)

4 oz (113 g) mixed nuts (hazelnut, almond, pistachio), sliced

4 oz (113 g) plain butter cookies, crumbled

Confectioners' sugar, for dusting

AN INDIAN FEAST

Achieving authenticity when cooking Indian food had always eluded me until I discovered Masala Mama and its charming owner, Nidhi. I don't like filling my cupboard with dozens of jars of spices that would go stale with barely a teaspoon used. If a recipe calls for ¼ teaspoon of this or ⅛ teaspoon of that, I would simply leave it out and I'm sure the recipe suffered as a result. The genius of Nidhi's lovingly prepared spice kits is that every pinch of hard-to-source spices is included in just the right proportions. I finally was able to make Indian food taste as complex, flavorful and authentic as I had experienced in India.

In late 2007, I took a month off work at Penguin and backpacked around India with one of my oldest and best friends, Claudia. I was a little nervous that ten years of corporate travel had turned me into a high-maintenance traveler. As it turned out, I could still happily rough it in $1-a-night "hotel" rooms with no electricity or hot water. For all my travels in Asia, nothing could have prepared me for India. To say I barely scratched the surface in four weeks of constant moving is a huge understatement. As we traveled from north to south, the menus changed dramatically and, as my heat tolerance grew, so did my courage in sampling unknown dishes.

With this menu, Nidhi has educated me even further. Nidhi moved to New York from Calcutta in 2003. Her family is originally from Rajasthan, while her husband is Punjabi, and she travels back several times a year. She has always been interested in food but it wasn't until she moved to New York and missed the flavors of home that she got really serious about cooking and eventually decided to start her business, creating spice kits and now sauces that make authentic Indian cuisine accessible to every home cook.

MENU

Spinach Dal with Garlic Tadka
by Masala Mama

Baigan Bharta
by Masala Mama

Tandoori Chicken
by Masala Mama

Kachumbar Raita
by Masala Mama

How to Make Perfect
Basmati Rice
by Masala Mama

Shrikhand (Sweet Yoghurt
with Saffron)
by Masala Mama

SPINACH DAL WITH GARLIC TADKA

by MASALA MAMA

Serves 4

Also called lahsuni palak dal, this lentil dish is super healthy and yet wonderfully flavorful. It gets its incredible zing from a magical Indian technique called tadka. Directly translated as "tempering," tadka is the process of adding spices to very hot ghee or oil and thereby releasing their aroma and flavor into the hot fat. This tempering is sometimes done at the very beginning or at the end of the cooking process. For this dal, it is traditionally prepared at the very last minute and added just before serving.

Heat the ghee in a medium to large saucepan over medium-high heat. Once hot, add the sliced shallots and cook until golden, about 5 minutes. Add the chopped tomatoes, ginger and green chile (if using) and cook, stirring occasionally, until the tomatoes are a little soft, about 3 minutes.

Add the drained lentils, 3 cups (710 ml) of water, ground turmeric and salt. Cook the lentils over high heat, uncovered at first. When the mixture comes to a boil, partially cover, lower the heat to medium and boil until the lentils are tender, about 20 minutes. (Make sure to watch the pot, as lentils have a tendency to overflow and create a mess.) Add ½ to 1 cup (118 to 237 ml) more water if the lentils absorb liquid too quickly. The mixture should have the consistency of pea soup.

When done, add the spinach and let it cook for a few minutes, until the spinach is soft. Adjust the salt to taste.

MAKE THE TADKA: Just before serving the dal, heat the ghee in a small skillet over medium-high heat. Once hot and shimmering (it's very important that the ghee be hot), add the cumin seeds, bay leaves and cardamom pods. The cumin will pop almost immediately. Let it sizzle until you see the spices getting darker, 30 to 60 seconds.

Add the garlic and asafoetida, stirring constantly to not let the garlic burn. Cook until garlic just barely gets a hint of color (this will happen very quickly). Add the red chili powder, give it one stir and immediately add to the dal.

NOTES: I like to slice my garlic with a mandoline, but even finely chopped garlic is fine.

Nidhi (and, indeed, Many Kitchens) now sells asafoetida (a.k.a. hing) in tiny jars, as it's hard to find and often varies in quality.

1 tbsp (15 g) ghee, unsalted butter or oil

2 medium-size shallots, sliced

2 tomatoes, peeled and chopped

1 (2" [5-cm]) piece fresh ginger, peeled and sliced

1 to 2 hot Indian green chiles, 1 serrano chile, or ½ jalapeño pepper, slit (optional)

1 cup (200 g) red lentils or masoor dal (pink lentils), washed well and drained

¼ tsp ground turmeric

½ tsp salt

2 big handfuls spinach, coarsely chopped

TADKA

2 tbsp (30 g) ghee

1 tsp cumin seeds

3 bay leaves

3 green cardamom pods, hand broken

3 to 4 medium-size garlic cloves, thinly sliced (see note)

¼ tsp asafoetida (see note)

½ tsp red chili powder

BAIGAN BHARTA
by MASALA MAMA

Serves 4

2 medium-size eggplants

3 tbsp (45 ml) vegetable oil

1 medium-size red onion, chopped
(about 1 cup [160 g])

1 or 2 hot Indian green chiles,
serrano chiles or jalapeño peppers,
chopped (the more seeds you
include, the hotter it will be)

2 to 3 tomatoes, blanched,
peeled and chopped

1 small bunch cilantro, chopped
(about ½ cup [20 g])

Salt

Baigan is eggplant and bharta means "mashed." In this quintessentially Punjabi dish, the eggplant is roasted on an open flame to create a unique smoky flavor and then mashed. It is simply delicious and a big favorite in Nidhi's home. Try it in the summer on the grill for an even smokier flavor.

The best way to roast the eggplant indoors is on a gas stovetop on an open flame. Begin by lining the area around the burners with foil to make cleanup much easier. Put the eggplants directly on two moderate flames and roast, turning every 4 to 5 minutes, until completely charred and the pulp is tender. If using the broiler, prick the eggplants a couple of times and put them on a foil-lined sheet pan under the boiler. Turn every 5 to 7 minutes, until completely charred. Let cool slightly, then peel the skin off and discard. Remove the stem at this time as well. Mash the pulp with a fork and set aside.

Heat the oil in a medium-size skillet over medium-high heat. Add the onion and green chiles and cook, stirring occasionally, until translucent, about 5 minutes. Add the tomatoes and cook for another few minutes, until soft. Add the mashed eggplant, cilantro and salt to taste. Cook for 5 to 7 minutes, taste for seasoning and serve hot!

TANDOORI CHICKEN
by MASALA MAMA

Serves 4

Another north Indian staple, for this dish the chicken is marinated overnight in a lovely blend of spices with yogurt and then traditionally grilled in clay oven or tandoor. It is still divinely tender and juicy when cooked under a broiler or on a barbecue, basted with butter and the leftover marinade that gives it a rich red hue.

MAKE THE MARINADE: Make a paste of the onion, ginger, garlic and lemon juice in a blender.

In a large bowl big enough to accommodate all the chicken, combine the paste with all the remaining ingredients of the marinade and mix well. Reserve 2 tablespoons (30 ml) of the marinade.

Make four or five deep diagonal slashes in each of the chicken pieces. Put the chicken in the remaining marinade, and using your hands, rub the marinade nicely into the chicken, making sure it goes into the gashes. Cover and refrigerate and allow to marinate for at least 2 hours and up to 12 hours.

When ready to cook, remove the chicken from the fridge and mix well with the marinade. Line a rimmed baking sheet with foil and set a wire rack on top. Arrange the chicken on the rack in a single layer, shaking off some of the excess marinade.

Preheat your broiler to high and position the rack 3 to 5 inches (7.5 to 13 cm) from the heat source. Broil the chicken until just cooked through and browned in spots, 7 to 10 minutes per side, basting with the butter and the reserved marinade as it starts drying out.

Alternatively, it is great prepared on a medium-high heat barbecue. Place the marinade-coated chicken on the barbecue. Grill the chicken until just cooked through, 7 to 10 minutes per side, basting with the butter and reserved marinade as it starts drying out.

Transfer the chicken to a platter. Garnish with the red onion, cilantro and lime wedges and serve right away.

MARINADE

½ small onion, peeled and sliced

1 (1" [2.5-cm]) piece fresh ginger, peeled and sliced

4 medium-size garlic cloves, peeled

1 tbsp (15 ml) freshly squeezed lemon juice

½ cup (122 g) Greek yogurt

1 tbsp (15 ml) oil

1 tsp salt

2 tbsp (12 g) tandoori masala

CHICKEN

1½ lb (680 g) bone-in chicken thighs and legs

2 tbsp (30 g) unsalted butter, melted

GARNISH

1 small red onion, thinly sliced crosswise and separated into rings

¼ cup (10 g) fresh cilantro

1 lime or lemon, cut into wedges

KACHUMBAR RAITA
by MASALA MAMA

Serves 4

1 small red onion, diced

6 grape tomatoes, quartered

1 Persian cucumber, diced

1 small bunch fresh cilantro, chopped (about ¼ cup [10 g])

2 cups (490 g) plain yogurt

Pinch of salt

Pinch of roasted ground cumin seeds

Pinch of red chili powder

Pinch of granulated sugar

Raita is an Indian condiment that is the perfect accompaniment to this menu. Combining the raita with kachumbar, a crunchy, tangy salad, makes for a deliciously fresh side that balances the heat of the other dishes.

Combine all the ingredients in a bowl and mix well. Adjust the salt to taste. Cover and refrigerate until ready to serve.

HOW TO MAKE PERFECT BASMATI RICE

by MASALA MAMA

Serves 4

There is nothing like perfectly cooked long-grain, fine-quality basmati rice to accompany a special Indian meal. Nidhi recommends putting the rice on 25 minutes before you're ready to eat so that you can serve it piping hot.

Wash the rice several times in cold water, as there is a lot of starch clinging to its grains. Soak it in about 5 cups (1.2 L) of water with ½ teaspoon of the salt for about 30 minutes.

Heat 3 cups (710 ml) of water to a boil in a heavy pan with a tight-fitting lid. Drain the rice and add to the boiling water along with the remaining ¼ teaspoon of salt and the ghee. Bring back to a boil, cover, lower the heat to low and cook for 16 minutes. Do not disturb the rice or take a peek while it's in the middle of cooking.

Turn off the heat and let the rice sit, covered, for another 5 to 7 minutes. Lift the cover and fluff gently with a fork.

Serve hot.

2 cups (420 g) uncooked basmati rice

¾ tsp salt

½ tsp ghee or unsalted butter

SHRIKHAND
by MASALA MAMA

Serves 4-6

2 cups (500 g) Greek-style yogurt

1 tbsp (15 ml) milk

½ tsp saffron threads

½ cup (96 g) granulated sugar

¼ tsp freshly ground green cardamom seeds, or to taste

TO SERVE

2 tbsp (21 g) chopped unsalted pistachios

2 tbsp (21 g) flaked or sliced almonds (optional)

Some saffron strands

Shrikhand, or saffron yogurt, is a perfect way to end an Indian meal. A light dessert from Gujarat, its vivid color and flavor comes from the gorgeous saffron. Wonderfully creamy and cooling after a meal filled with spices, it is finished off with nuts to add a little crunch.

Line a large sieve with cheesecloth. Place a bowl under the sieve and place the yogurt on the cloth. Cover and let it sit in the fridge for 5 to 6 hours.

Warm the milk (just needs to be warm, not hot) in a small pan or a microwave. In a small bowl, mix the saffron with the warm milk. Allow the saffron to infuse the milk for about 10 minutes, using the back of a spoon to crush the saffron further into the milk.

Remove the yogurt from the fridge (the liquid in the bowl below can be discarded). Sift the sugar into the thickened yogurt, then add the saffron milk and ground cardamom. Cover and chill in the fridge.

TO SERVE: Garnish with the pistachios, almonds (optional) and a few strands of saffron and serve cold in glasses or small saucers.

A PAN-ASIAN BANQUET

If it wasn't for my annual trips to Asia, I might very well have left publishing a lot sooner. Every January, I would head off on a three-week trip, visiting booksellers who had got to know me so well over the years that they would take me to get my gastronomic fixes, whether it was chile crab in Singapore, gyoza in Tokyo or sticky rice with mango in Bangkok. I miss those trips and the incredible diversity in cuisine not just from country to country, but from city to city. The best food was often found by the side of the road. I loved roaming the night markets to discover new treats.

Although it's impossible to include all the cuisines of Asia in one menu, I wanted to show the breadth of flavors that come from this extraordinary continent that I fell in love with while backpacking in the early '90s. Each country deserves a book, let alone a chapter of its own. At Many Kitchens, I'm fortunate enough to work with producers of Chinese, Korean and Vietnamese descent and their products showcase the very best of their heritages. Ken and Toan Huynh, the siblings behind the Saucey Sauce Co., contributed their own favorite ways to use two of their signature sauces, Spicy Garlic and Sweet Ginger. Edric Har from Brooklyn Wok Shop shows us how to make dumplings like a pro and crispy salmon cooked to perfection. Sandra Kim enlightens us on how to make kimchi with an American twist. We've also included a wonderful cocktail using matcha from Japan, from Sebastian Beckwith who has spent most of his adult life traveling through Asia, hunting down the rarest and most exquisite teas. It's a menu that reflects not only some of the amazingly diverse cultures of Asia, but also gives us a chance to collaborate with many of our talented producers and create a true potluck that's bursting with flavor.

MENU

Matcha Gimlet
by In Pursuit of Tea

Pork and Cabbage Dumplings
by Brooklyn Wok Shop

Vietnamese Savory Crêpes
with Spicy Garlic Sauce
by the Saucey Sauce Co.

Ginger Scallion Crispy Salmon
by Brooklyn Wok Shop

Sweet Ginger Pork Belly
by the Saucey Sauce Co.

Brussels Sprout Kimchi
over Soba Noodles
by Kyopo Kimchi

Sweet Sticky Rice with Mango
by Many Kitchens

MATCHA GIMLET
by IN PURSUIT OF TEA

Makes 1 or 2 cocktails

Matcha tea seems to have come into its own in the United States. The complexly flavored green powder that until recently you would only have found at a Japanese tea ceremony, is now being used to flavor everything from ice cream to cocktails. In Pursuit of Tea's Sebastian Beckwith worked with master mixologist Allen Katz to create this exotic and beautifully hued cocktail.

TO PREPARE THE SIMPLE SYRUP: In a small saucepan, bring 1 cup (237 ml) of water and the sugar to a boil and let simmer until the sugar is dissolved, about 3 minutes. Remove from the heat and let cool completely.

TO PREPARE THE MATCHA: In a cocktail shaker, combine the matcha tea with the filtered water. Shake vigorously until the powdered tea has completely dissolved.

TO PREPARE THE GIMLETS: Place all the ingredients in a cocktail shaker with some ice, shake vigorously and serve straight up.

SIMPLE SYRUP

1 cup (237 ml) water

1 cup (190 g) granulated sugar

MATCHA TEA

1 tbsp (6 g) Wakatake or good quality matcha tea

3 oz (90 ml) filtered water

GIMLET

1½ oz (44 ml) navy-strength gin

¾ oz (22 ml) freshly squeezed lime juice

½ oz (15 ml) simple syrup

¼ oz (7 ml) prepared matcha green tea

PORK AND CABBAGE DUMPLINGS
by BROOKLYN WOK SHOP

Makes 30 to 40 dumplings

12 oz (340 g) napa cabbage leaves

1 lb (453 g) ground pork

1 large egg

2 tbsp (30 ml) soy sauce

1 tsp salt

½ tsp freshly ground white pepper

1 tsp sesame oil

1 tsp granulated sugar

1 (12 oz [340 g]) package dumpling wrappers (I found the round ones very easy to work with)

DIPPING SAUCE

1 tbsp (15 ml) chili oil

1 tbsp (15 ml) soy sauce

Edric Har makes truly memorable dumplings. After culinary school and working in some of the most famous restaurants in New York, he and his wife Melissa opened a restaurant in Brooklyn serving what they like to call Chinese Food 2.0. Their dumplings and, in particular, their chili sauce developed such a cult following that they sold their restaurant to focus on their sauce. I have friends who go through it so fast that they always buy three at a time. You can find Edric at many of New York's markets, including the now hugely popular Smorgasburg.

Bring a large pot of water to a boil.

Rough chop the cabbage into ½-inch (1.3-cm) pieces and cook in the boiling water until tender, 3 to 4 minutes. Strain the cabbage and run under cold water to stop the cooking. When it's cool enough to handle, squeeze out the excess moisture.

In a large bowl, combine the pork, cabbage, egg, soy sauce, salt, white pepper, sesame oil and sugar. Mix well.

From here you can choose your favorite dumpling shape and begin to fold. A good beginner shape is the half-moon. Place about a tablespoon (15 g) of filling in the center of a round wrapper. Moisten the edges with water and fold in half, pressing the edges to seal the dumpling closed. Make sure you don't have any air pockets between the dumpling filling and the wrapper. You can have fun playing with different shapes. I found the easiest was a beggar's purse, where I set a spoonful of filling in the center of a round wrapper, then gathered the edges together and gave a little twist. I also wet my hands and ran them over the top to ensure that the purses stayed together as they were boiled.

Steam or boil the dumping until they are cooked through, 7 to 10 minutes. I found boiling to be the best way to ensure the filing was fully cooked and also the wrappers didn't become sticky while cooking.

Combine the dipping sauce ingredients and dip away!

VIETNAMESE SAVORY CRÊPES WITH SPICY GARLIC SAUCE

by THE SAUCEY SAUCE CO.

Makes 4 to 6 filled crepes

Lucky for Toan and her six siblings, her mother not only taught them how to make their family's traditional nuoc cham sauce, which is unbelievably tasty as well as versatile, but also the incredible street food she ate while growing up in Vietnam.

Their family favorite is panfried bánh xèo (bahn SAY-oh), savory Vietnamese crêpes. Made with chickpea flour, rice flour and coconut milk, they get their beautiful yellow color from the turmeric. Stuffed with slivers of pork, shrimp and bean sprouts, they are then wrapped in lettuce leaves and topped with fresh herbs such as mint, and dipped in the sauce company's signature nuoc cham for a savory, light and festive bite!

PREPARE THE CREPES: In a large bowl, mix the rice and chickpea and tapioca flours, sugar, salt and turmeric. Whisk in the coconut milk to make a thick batter, then slowly beat in enough water (about ½ cup [118 ml]) to make a very thin crêpe batter. It should drip from the ladle. Set aside to rest while preparing the filling.

PREPARE THE FILLING: In a wok or large sauté pan, heat 1 teaspoon of the oil over medium-high heat. Season the pork or chicken with salt and cook for 3 minutes. Add the garlic and shrimp and stir-fry until not quite cooked through, about another 3 minutes. Add the scallions, transfer to a bowl and cover to keep warm.

Heat about 1 tablespoon (15 ml) of the oil over medium-high heat in an 8- to 10-inch (20.5- to 25.5-cm) nonstick sauté pan or cast-iron skillet. Stir the crêpe batter well and pour one full ladle of batter into the hot pan, swirling to coat the bottom. The crêpe needs to be paper thin. It's a good idea to make a test crêpe to make sure your batter is the right consistency. When the center of the crêpe looks cooked through, bubbled up and the edges of the crêpe begin to brown, lower the heat to low and sprinkle a small handful of bean sprouts and the shrimp mixture over half of the crêpe and cover for 30 seconds. Fold over the crêpe to cover the filling and slide onto a plate. Repeat until you've made enough crêpes, adding 1 tablespoon (15 ml) of olive oil to the pan before adding each ladle of batter.

(continued)

VIETNAMESE CRÊPE BATTER

½ cup (76 g) rice flour

½ cup (76 g) chickpea flour

1 tbsp (10 g) tapioca flour

½ tsp granulated sugar

½ tsp salt

¼ tsp ground turmeric

1 cup (237 ml) coconut milk

CRÊPE FILLING

4 to 6 tbsp (59 to 79 ml) olive oil

8 oz (227 g) pork or chicken, thinly sliced

Salt

2 garlic cloves, minced

12 oz (340 g) shrimp, peeled and deveined

2 to 3 tbsp (5 to 7 g) scallions, sliced

1 lb (450 g) bean sprouts

VIETNAMESE SAVORY CRÊPES WITH SPICY GARLIC SAUCE (continued)

MAKE THE SPICY GARLIC SAUCE: Combine all the ingredients, stir and shake very well.

TO SERVE: Break off a piece of crêpe, add a mint leaf and place it in a lettuce leaf. Then roll up the lettuce and dip away in the spicy garlic sauce.

SPICY GARLIC SAUCE

Juice of ½ lime (about 1 tbsp [15 ml])

3 tbsp (38 g) granulated sugar

1 tsp rice vinegar (optional)

½ cup (118 ml) Asian fish sauce, or more for extra fish sauce depth

½ cup (118 ml) water

⅓ cup (54 g) minced garlic

1 tsp Thai (bird's eye) chile, or to taste

FOR SERVING

Lettuce leaves

Fresh mint leaves

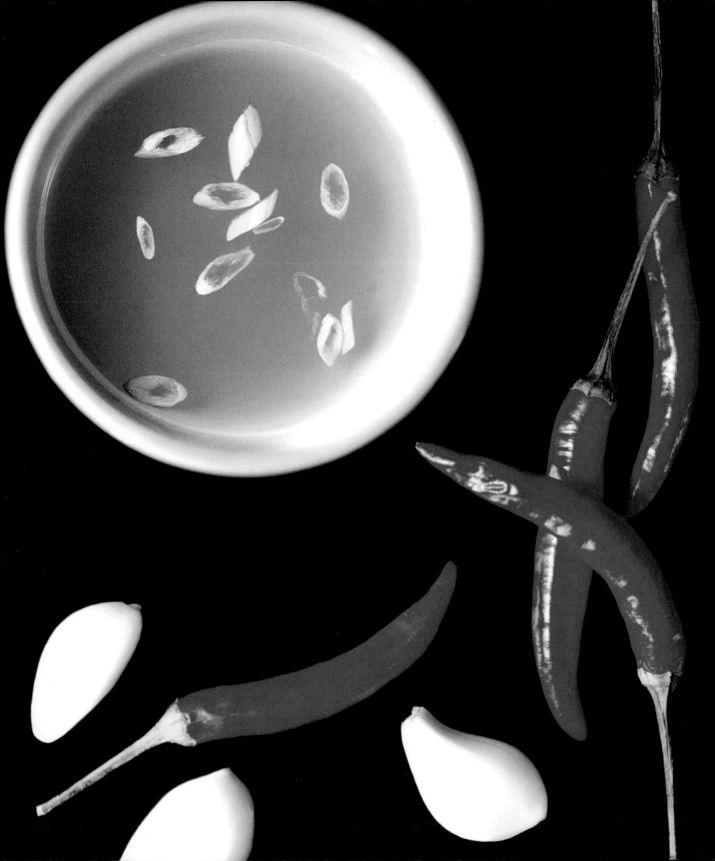

GINGER SCALLION
CRISPY SALMON
by BROOKLYN WOK SHOP

Serves 6

6 tbsp (90 ml) vegetable oil

6 (6 oz [170 g]) pieces salmon, skin on

Salt

Freshly ground white pepper

6 tbsp (86 g) fresh ginger, cut into matchsticks

6 scallions, chopped

1 tbsp (15 ml) soy sauce

I had never managed to get that perfect crisp skin and velvety interior when I cooked salmon at home. Edric's method will make you feel like a professional chef and is a perfect example of his "Chinese Food 2.0" blending of classic Chinese ingredients with time-honored French techniques.

Preheat the oven to 400°F (204°C).

In a nonstick pan, heat 4 tablespoons (60 ml) of the vegetable oil over high heat until it shimmers. Season the salmon with salt and pepper, then add to the hot pan, skin side down. Lower the heat to medium. After 3 to 4 minutes, the skin will begin to crisp and brown. If your pan has a heatproof handle, place in the oven and bake for 7 to 10 minutes, or to your desired doneness (keep the fish skin side down). (Tip: Insert a paring knife into the center of the salmon and then touch the tip of the knife to your hand. If it feels room temperature, the salmon is done.) If your pan doesn't have a heatproof handle, transfer the salmon to a baking sheet, skin side up and bake for 7 to 10 minutes. Remove the salmon from the oven and place, skin side up, on a plate.

Heat the remaining 2 tablespoons (30 ml) of oil in a small pot until it begins to smoke, then remove from the heat.

Place the ginger matchsticks and scallions on top of the salmon and spoon the hot oil over them to flash cook the ginger and scallion. Pour soy sauce over the fish and serve.

SWEET GINGER PORK BELLY
by THE SAUCEY SAUCE CO.

Serves 6

Pork is an essential ingredient in Vietnamese cuisine—almost as important as the almighty cow (to make pho!). Aside from being used in such classic delicious Vietnamese dishes as com suong nuong (pork chops with broken rice) and bún bò hue (tangy pork broth noodle soup), pork belly is a luxurious ingredient meant to be cooked with the best ingredients. Ken shares his favorite version made with his company's incredible sweet ginger glaze.

MAKE THE GINGER GLAZE: Mix all the ingredients, plus ½ cup (118 ml) of water, in a saucepan and bringing to a slow boil. After 5 to 10 minutes, you should achieve a thicker consistency.

PREPARE THE PORK: In a bowl, mix ½ cup (118 ml) of the glaze with 2 teaspoons (10 g) of salt and 1 teaspoon of black pepper in a bowl. Rub the pork with the mixture, making sure to get in all the folds. Cover with plastic wrap and refrigerate for at least 4 hours, or overnight.

Preheat the oven to 450°F (232°C).

Rub 1 teaspoon of the oil over the top of the skin of the pork belly, sprinkle with the remaining ½ cup (118 ml) of the glaze as well as more salt and pepper and rub in, pour the remaining teaspoon of oil over the glaze and then really rub this into the skin so that everything gets in between the skin and down onto the meat.

Peel the onions, cut into large pieces and add to a roasting dish. Place the seasoned pork belly, skin side up, on the bed of onions and then put into the oven. Roast for 10 to 15 minutes, or until the skin of the belly starts to bubble and is golden brown. Once it is sufficiently crackled, turn the oven temperature down to 325°F (162°C), then roast for 1½ to 2 hours, covering with foil to retain moisture. Remove the meat carefully from the oven and test to see whether it pulls apart easily. If not, put it back in the oven until the meat is ready, then remove from the oven. If you want a bit more of a crackly pork skin, turn over the pork belly and leave in for another 15 minutes, uncovered, but monitor closely.

Once the pork is cooked sufficiently, place on a wooden board and allow to rest.

Slice into thick pieces, garnish with the scallions and serve.

GINGER GLAZE (MAKES ABOUT 8 OZ [237 ML])

Juice of ½ lime (about 1 tbsp [15 ml])

4 tbsp (48 g) granulated sugar

1 tsp rice vinegar (optional)

½ cup (118 ml) Asian fish sauce, or more for extra fish sauce depth

¼ cup (57 g) minced fresh ginger

2 tsp (4 g) tapioca flour

Salt and pepper

PORK BELLY

1 (6 lb [2.7kg]) slab pork belly, skin on

2 tsp (10 g) salt

1 tsp freshly ground black pepper

2 tsp (10 ml) olive oil

3 onions

½ cup (20 g) chopped scallions, for garnish

BRUSSELS SPROUT KIMCHI OVER SOBA NOODLES
by KYOPO KIMCHI

Makes 4 cups (320 g)

KIMCHI

- 2 lb (907 g) Brussels sprouts
- 3 tbsp (45 g) kosher salt, plus more as needed for seasoning
- 5 oz (142 g) carrots, finely julienned
- 8 oz (227 g) daikon radish, finely julienned
- ⅓ cup (54 g) fresh ginger, minced
- 2 tbsp (20 g) garlic, minced
- ¼ cup (40 g) jalapeño pepper, minced
- ½ cup (80 g) thinly sliced (on bias) scallions, green and white parts
- ⅓ cup (80 ml) soy sauce
- 5 oz (150 ml) rice vinegar
- 3½ oz (100 g) coarse Korean chili flakes (see note)
- 1½ tbsp (5 g) bonito flakes

SOBA NOODLES

- 8 oz (240 g) uncooked soba noodles
- 2 tbsp (30 ml) sesame oil
- ½ cup (80 g) small-diced firm tofu
- ½ cup (80 g) seeded and finely julienned cucumber
- 1 tbsp (10 g) black sesame seeds, toasted
- 2 tbsp (7 g) scallions, thinly sliced on bias

Sandra Kim decided to name her company after the term used to describe *Korean Americans: Kyopo. Having grown up in California and worked in top New York City restaurants, she has updated the kimchi she learned to make from her parents with more American ingredients. Her vibrant Brussels sprout kimchi is a perfect example of how she blends her two cultures.*

PREPARE THE KIMCHI: Using a mandoline, slice the Brussels sprouts vertically into ⅛-inch (3-mm) slices (please be sure to use the guard and keep your fingers safe!). In a stainless-steel mixing bowl, mix the Brussels sprouts and salt together until fully incorporated. Allow to sit for at least 2 hours.

Add the carrots, radish, ginger, garlic, jalapeño and scallions and mix well with the Brussels sprouts. Add the soy sauce, rice vinegar, chili flakes, bonito flakes and 1 cup (237 ml) of water. Mix everything together and adjust the seasoning as needed.

Allow the mixture to sit for 30 minutes, covered with plastic wrap; taste and add salt as needed. Transfer the kimchi to a glass jar, pushing down firmly to remove any air bubbles, leaving at least a 1-inch (2.5-cm) headspace. Place in a cool room-temperature space for 10 to 12 hours for fermentation process to begin before putting in the refrigerator. Kimchi should be immersed in its juices and liquids when jarred. The kimchi will be ready to eat in a few days and will continue to improve over time.

PREPARE THE SOBA NOODLES: Cook the soba noodles as directed by the package instructions. Once drained, toss in the sesame oil and place on a parchment-lined sheet pan to cool, mixing every few minutes to make sure the noodles do not stick together.

ASSEMBLE THE DISH: Once the noodles are cooled, transfer them to a mixing bowl, toss the noodles with 1 cup (145 g) of the kimchi, ¼ cup (60 ml) of the kimchi juice and the tofu and cucumber. Garnish with the sesame seeds and scallions.

NOTE: Korean chili is much milder and worth finding, as there is no equal substitute.

SWEET STICKY RICE WITH MANGO
by MANY KITCHENS

Serves 6

Sticky rice is my favorite dessert after a spicy meal in Thailand. I always find room for it at the end of every meal and make sure to have one last taste at Bangkok's Suvarnabhumi Airport before boarding the plane home. Sweet and sticky rice with luxurious fresh mango, it is filling but never heavy. Missing Thailand over the years, I've learned how how to make it at home.

Rinse the rice in a sieve under running water and then soak in water overnight in a covered bowl.

Drain and rinse again under running water in a heatproof sieve. Bring a pot of water to a boil and steam the rice by placing the sieve above the water level and covering the pot and sieve. Steam for 20 to 30 minutes, until cooked. Transfer the rice to a bowl.

In a small saucepan, bring 1 cup (237 ml) of the coconut milk, ⅓ cup (64 g) of the sugar and the salt to a boil, stirring continuously until the sugar has completely dissolved. Add the liquid to the rice and mix well. Cover and leave for an hour, or until all the coconut milk has been absorbed.

When ready to serve, heat the remaining ½ cup (118 ml) of coconut milk, the reserved cream, if you had any, and the remaining 3 tablespoons (32 g) of sugar in the same saucepan and bring to a boil as you did before, stirring until all the sugar has dissolved.

To serve, fill a ½ cup (118 ml) mold or measuring cup with the rice and pat down slightly. Invert onto a plate; the rice should slip out easily. Continue to mold the rice until you have six individual servings. Pour some of the sweetened milk on top of the rice as well as sprinkling on black sesame seeds and serve with sliced mango.

1½ cups (315 g) uncooked glutinous white rice (also called sticky rice, sweet rice or waxy rice)

1½ cups (355 ml) coconut milk (reserve any thick cream from top of can)

½ cup (96 g) granulated sugar

¼ tsp salt

1 tbsp (10 g) black sesame seeds

2 large mangoes, peeled, pitted and thinly sliced

ACKNOWLEDGMENTS

First and foremost, my eternal gratitude to all the producers who so generously contributed their recipes and patiently answered my questions; you made this book a reality.

They say it takes a village, but in this case, it feels more like a city; I have called on so many friends who have donated everything from time and talent to a treasure trove of props. Thank you to Kate Stark, Camille Sweeney, Kate Tyler, Devin Luna, Lydia Hurt, Betty Kramer, Cree LeFavour, Circe Hamilton, Alina Gozin'a, Ben Pentreath, Hal Fessenden, Mamie Healey, Christopher Sweet, Linda LeHardy Sweet and Connie Dickson.

To everyone who has helped me follow my dream in creating Many Kitchens, most notably my family, Eliot and Roly Nolen, Richard and Priscilla Hunt, Debbie DeCotis, Sam and Sally Butler, Leigh Butler, Henry and Leslie Astor, Tim Bradley and Lolly Nolen; thank you for believing in me.

Thank you also to everyone at Page Street Publishing, the sales department at Macmillan and Kim Yorio at YC Media.

And most important, to Aurora Satler; this book is as much yours as it is mine.

PHOTO CREDITS

Alina Gozin'a: pages 6, 16, 19, 26, 33, 71, 85, 86, 109, 123, 129, 138, 141, 146, 149, 153, 161, 166, 171, 175, 178, 181

Circe Hamilton: pages 12, 15, 24, 68, 72, 76, 80, 15

Phillip Romano: page 56

All photo editing by Brittainy Dale

ABOUT THE AUTHOR

Valentina Rice is the founder of manykitchens.com, a curated online marketplace for artisanal foods. Before founding Many Kitchens, Valentina was vice president of International Sales and Marketing at Penguin Books. Connect with Valentina on her blog at Many Kitchens and watch her TEDxtalk on "Why Competition Is So Last Century." She lives in New York City while curating foods from around the world.

INDEX